The Only True Biography of Benjamin Franklin

🐾 🐾 🐾

By His Cat, Missy Hooper

🐾 🐾 🐾

(With Hardly Any Help From Dan Greenburg)

THE ONLY TRUE BIOGRAPHY OF BENJAMIN FRANKLIN

🐾 🐾 🐾

BY HIS CAT, MISSY HOOPER

🐾 🐾 🐾

(With Hardly Any Help From Dan Greenburg)

Copyright © Dan Greenburg 2019

Cover by J. Brent Hill
Published by ThunderStone Books

This book may not be reproduced in whole or in part, in any form or by any means, electronic or mechanical, including photocopying, recording, or by any information storage and retrieval system now known or hereafter invented, without written permission from the publisher.

978-1-63411-010-5 (ISBN 13)

Foreword
By Dan Greenburg

Although I've lived with a large black-and-white cat and a tiny gray one for years, it was only recently and quite by accident I discovered (1) that cats can actually speak human languages if they want to and (2) that the Feline Historical Society has been keeping secret records of all human historical events for several centuries.

One of these historical records is The Only True Biography of Ben Franklin. It was written by his cat, Missy Hooper, and has been translated from the original Cattish by members of the Feline Historical Society.

Cats who kept records for the Feline Historical Society at first thought they could write by catching birds and using the ends of their feathers as quill pens. But unlike humans, cats don't have thumbs to grip pens, so they ended up dipping their claws directly into ink and writing. They learned to let one of their claws grow longer to write with. If you ever see a cat with one claw longer than the others and the claw is black at the tip, chances are the cat is a member of the Feline Historical Society.

I took the liberty of modernizing Missy's language after it had been translated, to make it more readable. Cattish is not a difficult language for humans to learn, though. Let me give you an example.

<u>Quotation from the Cattish</u>: Meow mowr rare fffft prowl yaw.

<u>Translation into English</u>: Meow means Hello, goodbye or peace. Mowr means I was. Rare means feeling upset. Fffft means mad. Prowl means I'm better. Yaw means feed me NOW. So: "Meow mowr rare fffft prowl yaw" means "Hello, I was feeling upset and mad before, but I'm better—feed me NOW."

If you'd like to try reading Missy's story in the original Cattish, you can contact the Feline Historical Society Museum in Katoomba, Australia.

FOREWORD
By Missy Hooper

My name is Missy Hooper, and I'm a large black-and-white cat. I am certainly not fat, as some unkind people have suggested. These people have always been jealous of my relationship with Dr. Franklin.

Dr. Franklin and I worked together for a great many years. I taught him many things he didn't know. He taught me many things, some of which I didn't know and some of which I forgot I knew. Together we changed the course of history.

The story of the American War of Independence is the story of Dr. Franklin and me. All of America's Founding Fathers played an important role in the formation of the United States. But to be honest, Ben Franklin was the most important of all the Founding Fathers, and he always told me he could never have done what he did without my help. Let's face it—without us, the United States of America would still be a British colony. I think you'll see that once I tell you how Ben and I convinced France to join the Colonists in the War of Independence. If you don't see that, you weren't paying attention.

Most of the cats who have written biographies of their humans for the Feline Historical Society are members of the rare Catus Longevus breed. Our members can live as long as 90 years. Those biographers who lived a normal cat lifespan were tragically unable to complete their work. Although I am now too old to do more than sit in the sun and scratch away at my memoirs, there was a time when I was considered one of the wittiest, fluffiest cats in Philadelphia.

In the stories that follow I'll be quoting a number of people. I'd like to point out that what I have them saying is what they intended, but not exactly what they said. I can't be expected to remember every single word that anybody ever spoke in my presence.

CHAPTER 1

Ben Meets Me, I Learn about Aphorisms, and the Adventure Begins

Don't ask what I was doing that morning in 1729, racing down a narrow alley in Philadelphia, wearing kitten mittens, chasing a small brown field mouse. It had something to do with jumping up on a hot stove the day before. It had something to do with the fact that mittens protect sore paws.

Anyway, I was in hot pursuit of this nasty little rodent and getting closer every second. As we tore around the corner, the mouse ran smack into a large sheepdog. The mouse screeched to a stop, turned quickly around, and headed back in my direction.

As the mouse passed me, I pounced. I landed with both front paws on his back. But since I was wearing mittens, I couldn't get a grip on him. He wriggled out of my grasp and took off down the alley.

"Hmm," said a voice behind me. "How interesting. A cat wearing gloves catches no mice."

I looked around. Standing behind me was a young

human. He had long wavy hair, but he was already growing bald above his forehead. He wore wire-rimmed glasses and a smudged printer's apron. He looked about 23 in human years. He was writing in a small notebook.

"Excuse me?" I said.

"I said, 'A cat wearing gloves catches no mice,'" said the young man. "By the way, you didn't actually speak to me, did you?"

"I certainly did," I said. "And if you look closely, you'll see that I'm actually wearing mittens."

"Hmm," he said, making another note. "A cat who keeps her paws warm and speaks. I hadn't realized that cats could speak."

"Well, we can," I said. "We know whatever language the local humans speak. What is your interest in cats wearing gloves?"

"Do you know what an aphorism is?" he asked.

"Of course," I said. "An aphorism is a wise thought in a short sentence. Why?"

"Well, I'm a printer. I've been collecting aphorisms for years. Someday I'll print them in a book. And you've just given me another one: A cat wearing gloves catches no mice. It means if you don't use everything you've got, you won't be successful. By the way, my name is Ben Franklin."

"Missy Hooper," I said, shaking paws with him. "And you didn't hear me. What I'm wearing are mitttens. Do you have any better aphorisms than that one?"

"Yes," said Ben. "What do you think of this? Fish and visitors stink in three days."

"Well, being a cat," I said, "I happen to like stinky fish. The stinkier the better, in fact. But most visitors stink after only one day, because humans bathe hardly at all. And they don't even know how to lick themselves clean, which even the dumbest cat in the world knows how to do."

"Hmm," said Ben. "So you're saying that these aphorisms of mine . . ."

". . . need a lot of work," I said. "Frankly, Ben, you could use somebody to help you write them. Which I'd be perfectly happy to do, in exchange for room and board."

"Take off the gloves, throw in mouse-catching, and you've got yourself a deal," he said.

"Good," I said, "I'll take off my MITTENS and throw in mouse-catching."

So that is how I began living and working with Ben Franklin.

Chapter 2

Ben Starts Telling about His Childhood, but Sadly We Have to Stop

Before Ben tells me about his childhood, I should explain that his family was better off than colonists who lived on farms rather than in cities. Colonists who lived on farms had to make most of the things they owned. They built barns and small log cabins themselves, some with no more than one large room, some with dirt floors, and most heated only by a fireplace.

Women made soap from lye, water, and fireplace ashes. They spun flax into thread, and wool into yarn, and they sewed the family's clothes. Children as young as four years old hauled water from nearby streams, milked cows, churned cream into butter, and kept cows and chickens from eating the crops.

Children lucky enough to go to school went to a one-room schoolhouse where one teacher taught all grades. Instead of writing on paper, they used small chalkboards called slates. Store-bought toys were rare, so they made their own. Instead of a bathroom they had an outhouse near the cabin and used leaves or dried cornhusks for toilet paper.

Ben's family was better off than most because they were tradesmen—a printer, a blacksmith, and a soap and candle maker.

Shortly after I moved in with Ben, he bought a newspaper that was going out of business. He renamed it The Pennsylvania Gazette.

"I'm going to add jokes, gossip and aphorisms," he said. "People love aphorisms. I've got a new one for you, Missy: 'If your head is wax, don't walk in the sun.'"

"If your head is made of wax," I said, "you've got bigger problems than whether or not to walk in the sun."

"All right," he said, "then what about this: 'A spoonful of honey will catch more flies than a gallon of vinegar.'"

"Why would you want to catch flies?" I said. "They taste awful. I'd rather catch mice, which are a lot tastier."

Ben sighed and shook his head. "Never mind," he said.

It turned out Ben was right. People loved the aphorisms. And people loved the new Pennsylvania Gazette. Ben started making lots of money. That gave me an idea.

"You're doing what?" said Ben. "Starting a newspaper for cats?"

"I'm calling it The Philadelphia Feline. I've talked to several important cats in the neighborhood. They'll buy it. I'll have serious information: The best places in Philadelphia to catch certain types of birds. Places in Philadelphia where catnip grows wild, and addresses of homes with dangerous dogs . . ."

"You'll have entertainment features, too?"

"Absolutely," I said. "Like 'My Most Embarrassing Moment': You jump gracefully up to a high shelf, but you miss the edge and crash to the floor. You start casually licking your shoulder and pretend that's what you intended to do in the first place. That one happens to all of us, of course. It's just fun to see a cat admit it in print."

"Missy, are you doing this newspaper to copy me?" Ben asked.

"Of course, I am," I said. "I'm also going to do interviews. My readers would be interested in your life story. Would you be my first interview?"

"Well, I'm pretty busy working on The Pennsylvania Gazette."

"I know, but it won't take long. Do you have a minute to talk right now?"

"Right now?" he said. "I don't know. How long

would you need?"

"Not more than a couple of minutes," I said. "First, where were you born?"

"Well, I was born in Boston, in a house on Milk Street, on January 17, 1706. Boston is the largest town in North America. It is considerably larger than either Philadelphia or New York. Strangers who come to Boston are shown more hospitality and kindness than in either Philadelphia or New York. The best street in Boston is King's Street, which runs down to Long Wharf and Boston Harbor. There are more than 100 large ships in Boston Harbor, did you know that?"

"I don't care about Boston," I said. "Tell me about you."

"All right. I was the fifteenth and youngest son of seventeen children. Now here's something your readers will find interesting: Not only was I my father's youngest son, but my father was his father's youngest son. And my grandfather was his father's youngest son. And my great grandfather was his father's youngest son. And my great-great grandfather was his father's youngest son. Isn't that interesting?"

"Not to hurt your feelings," I said, "but humans would probably find that more interesting than cats. What does your family do?"

"Well, my brother James is a printer, my father is a soap and candle maker, and my brother Samuel is a blacksmith. My father hoped I'd grow up to be a minister."

"A minister?" I said. "Why?"

"Well, I was very smart, Missy. I started reading at a very young age."

"Uh huh," I said. "Well, I started walking three weeks after I was born. A little wobbly, but I was walking. How many humans can do that? Did you go to school?"

"Yes. Because my father wanted me to become a minister, he put me in Latin school when I was eight. I was terrible at mathematics, but good at Latin and Greek and everything else, especially writing."

"Gracko," I said.

"What?"

"Gracko. It means congratulations in Cattish, our native language."

"I had no idea there was a Cattish language," he said.

"Oh, it's a beautiful, romantic language," I said. "Much more complex than Doggish, which is mostly either greetings or warnings—woof-woof, ruff-ruff, arf-arf—that sort of thing."

"I speak five languages besides English," he said. "I taught myself French, Latin, Italian, Spanish, and

German. Could you teach me to speak Cattish?"

"I don't know," I said. "Let me give you a little test. Does 'Meow' mean 'Hello', 'Goodbye', or 'Peace'?"

"Hello," he said.

"No, it's all three," I said. "Does 'squeek-squeek' mean 'mouse' or 'wagon wheel'?"

"Mouse," he said.

"Right," I said. "OK, here's a short sentence in Cattish: 'Meer browr merff?' Does that mean 'Who wants to know?' or 'My brother is dead'?"

"'My brother is dead,'" he said.

"No, it's 'Who wants to know?'" I said. "Well, that's only one out of three. You're not as good at languages as you think. Getting back to our interview, how many years did you go to school?"

"Well," he said, "these days hardly any children go to school. They work 12 to 14 hours a day, six days a week. Children are considered tiny adults and they're expected to learn a trade and earn a living, not to waste time going to school. Besides, school is expensive. My father took me out of school after two years. The moment he realized I was never going to be a minister."

"What made him realize that?"

Ben laughed.

"Funny story," he said. "My father always insists

on saying very long prayers before and after meals. They bore me silly. So one day my mother had just sealed up a barrel of salted meat that we would be eating over the winter. All I could think about was how many times that winter my father would have to say grace over the meat in that barrel. I said, 'Father, I have a wonderful time-saving idea. Why don't you just say grace over the whole barrel right now?' He took me out of school the very next day."

"And that's when you learned to become a printer?"

"No," said Ben. "First he taught me how to make soap and candles. But I hated the smell of the hot wax and the boiling soap, so when I was 12 he made me an apprentice to my brother James, the printer. Do you know anything about apprentices?"

"Not really," I said.

"Apprentices work for a tradesman and learn his trade, but they're more slaves than employees. They're given meals and a place to stay, but no pay. When you become an apprentice, you sign a paper promising to obey your master until you're 21 years old. And masters beat their apprentices whenever they do anything wrong. James beat me lots more than the other apprentices."

"To show he wasn't giving you special treatment?" I asked.

"Exactly. Printing is a slow process, Missy. Every letter, every punctuation mark, every space between words, is a separate piece of metal type that you have to put in place by hand. I learned to set type and run the printing press very quickly, and then I got bored. I tried to teach myself other things to keep from being bored. I devoured every book I could find."

"What kind of books?"

"I read books on writing and taught myself how to write essays and poetry. I read the classic books of English literature. Then I copied them down, cut them apart, rearranged them, and put them together again. Sometimes I rewrote them. Sometimes I liked what I had rewritten better than the originals."

"I always like what I write better than what others wrote," I said.

"Uh huh. I read a French book about swimming. The book described 40 different strokes. I taught myself all 40 strokes and more. I taught myself to swim without using my hands. I taught myself to swim without using my feet. I taught myself to swim with both of my legs tied together. I taught myself to swim while holding my right leg in my left hand."

"I hate swimming," I said. "All cats do. We're great swimmers, but we hate the water. Except for tigers, of course. Tigers love the water. Isn't that strange?"

"It is," he said. "It's also strange that hardly any

humans these days besides me know how to swim. Anyway, I decided I might be able to swim faster if I tied wooden paddles to my hands and feet. Exhausting! Next, I decided to fly a kite while floating on my back, and let the kite pull me across the water. That did work."

"Why did you want a kite to pull you?" I asked. "Because you're lazy?"

Ben scratched his head. "Hmm. I think I'm an odd combination of lazy and not lazy. I work extra hard inventing things that will allow me to work less hard. Anyway, next I read a book on how to argue. The book said never contradict someone and tell him he's wrong. The book said it's better to ask clever questions of the person you're arguing with and trick him into contradicting himself."

"Mmm," I said, yawning, and stretching my back. "Well, Ben, I'm afraid we have to stop now."

"I thought you wanted to get my whole life story for the interview."

"I do," I said. "It's just that I need a break right now."

"Oh, sure," he said. "Well, let me know when you want to pick it up again."

CHAPTER 3

A Difficult Kittenhood in the Shadow of Fluffy

All right, you're probably tired of hearing about Ben. I know you're anxious to hear about me.

I was the biggest in a litter of five black-and-white kittens. Our mother's name was Mrs. Hooper. If she had a first name, she didn't tell us. She insisted that we kittens call her Mrs. Hooper instead of Mom. To tell you the truth, she wasn't the warmest of cat mothers.

All of us kittens were black with white markings, but Fluffy was the only one with perfect markings. She had perfect little white paws, a perfect white chest like a ruffled formal shirt, and a perfect white triangle above her perfect pink nose.

Fluffy had the loudest meow, so she got the most milk. Everybody thought Fluffy was the most beautiful kitten and everybody liked her best. I'm the kitten who everybody said had a great personality. The one who was so much fun to talk to. Meaning the one who wasn't good-looking.

    Did I care that Fluffy was the best looking one of my sisters and brothers and that she got all the attention? I did not. I had my books, I had my writing, and I had my collection of miniature mouse skulls, and that was quite enough for me. And if you believe that, you're a lot more gullible than I thought. Gullible means willing to believe anything anybody tells you. Don't worry, I used to be gullible myself.

Chapter 4

Ben Pretends to Be a Cranky Middle-Aged Widow, Is Cheated by the Governor of Pennsylvania, and Is Stranded in London without a Penny

"All right, Ben," I said. "Let's continue your interview. Where did we stop?"

"I was telling you about being an apprentice for my brother James, the printer."

"Oh, right," I said. "What did you print? Books? Magazines? Money?"

"James published a newspaper called the New-England Courant. I was now 16, and I thought it might be fun to write letters to the newspaper under a made-up name. In my letters I pretended to be a cranky, middle-aged widow named Mrs. Silence Dogood. I slipped my letters under the print shop door at night. James thought they were from a real person. He published every one of them."

"Didn't he recognize your handwriting?"

"I disguised my handwriting," said Ben. "Anyway, Silence Dogood became famous in Boston.

Everyone was dying to know who she was. I had to bite my tongue so hard to keep from laughing that my tongue almost bled."

"Did James ever find out you were the one who wrote them?" I asked.

Ben nodded, chuckling. "He was furious. He beat me, of course."

"Why?"

"Maybe he felt I'd tricked him. Maybe he'd liked my letters and he was embarrassed to find they'd been written by his little brother. Anyway, I hated being beaten. I hated being an apprentice. Even though I'd signed a paper promising to be his apprentice till I was 21, I couldn't stand it anymore. When I was 17, I ran away."

"Where to? Philadelphia?"

"No, first to New York. It was three days by boat from Boston to New York, but that was still faster than horse and carriage. The only printer in New York couldn't give me a job, so I left."

"I myself have never been to New York," I said, "but I hear it's a real mess. Dirt roads that become mud banks when it rains. Pigs wallowing in the mud. Raw sewage with human poop running down the middle of the streets. Pee-yew!"

"I went next to Philadelphia," Ben continued. "That's a five-day trip by boat and foot. I had to walk

50 miles in New Jersey in a heavy rain just to get to the boat that would take me to Philadelphia. When I got to Philadelphia I was a wreck. So wet and filthy! Dirty socks and underpants were hanging out of my pockets. I was exhausted. I had very little money. I was starving."

"Why did you have dirty socks and underpants hanging out of your pockets?" I asked.

"Because I didn't own a suitcase," he said. "In a bakery I bought three tremendously long loaves of bread. I tucked a loaf under each arm and munched on the third one as I walked down the street. A pretty girl saw me and giggled at the sight of this wet, filthy boy, munching three loaves of bread."

"She was probably giggling at your dirty underpants," I said.

"Perhaps," he said. "The streets were filthy and full of rubbish. The heat was unbearable because the sun's rays were reflecting off all the brick houses. Most people in Philadelphia had awnings over their doors and windows to shield them from the sun. At sunset they threw bucketsful of water on the pavement."

"To wash off the filth and rubbish?" I asked.

"No, to cool it off," he said. "The next day I got cleaned up. I not only found a job as a printer, I found a place to live with a family named Read. That

night at dinner I met the Reads' daughter, Deborah. The moment I saw her, I burst out laughing. Deborah Read was the same pretty girl who had giggled at me the day before!"

"So, did you fall in love with her?" I asked.

"No, no. But Debby is a really nice girl. Very, very sensible. When we met, she was only 15."

"How old were you?"

"Seventeen," he said. "She'll make somebody a

good wife someday."

"Somebody like you?" I asked.

"No ma'am!" he said. "I don't ever intend to get married."

"Why not?"

"It would limit me too much," he said. "I have too many interests. Anyway, where was I? Oh yes. As soon as I'd saved up some money working at the print shop, I bought a fancy collection of clothes and went back to visit my family in Boston."

"Did you see James?"

"Oho! Definitely!" he said. "I dropped in at his print shop—not to apologize for running away, but to show off my newly-earned wealth." Ben laughed. "The apprentices were very jealous."

"And James?"

"James was furious. Furious!" Ben laughed. "But I wasn't his apprentice anymore, so he couldn't beat me. I went back to Philadelphia. When I was 18, I met Sir William Keith, the governor of Pennsylvania. Governor Keith was impressed by my writing and my printing. He offered me the job of printing all of Pennsylvania's official papers. All I had to do was buy a printing press."

"Aren't presses horribly expensive?" I asked.

"Horribly," said Ben. "Governor Keith said he'd lend me the money to buy one, but no presses can be bought in the Colonies. I would have to go to England for that."

"Why can't you buy a press in the Colonies?" I asked.

"England insists on selling us all things like printing presses themselves. To make sure we don't get too independent. Anyway, was I ever excited! What a chance for an 18-year-old boy—to have the governor give me the job of printing all of Pennsylvania's official papers. To go all the way to London to get it!"

"Weren't you scared to go all the way to London alone?" I asked.

"Not really. So Governor Keith promised to give me the money to buy the press, but it wouldn't be in cash. It would be in the form of a letter, which I could cash at the governor's bank in London as soon as I got there. The annoying thing was that every time I came by the governor's office to get the letter, he was too busy to write it. Each time, I was promised that the next time I came by, it would be ready for sure."

"And you believed him?" I asked.

"Well, he was the governor, Missy. The letter still wasn't ready the day before I went to England, but Governor Keith promised he'd send it to the ship before we sailed. It would be given to me as soon as the ship reached England. I boarded the London Hope and we sailed for England."

"What was the voyage like?" I asked.

"I had never sailed that far before. The London Hope, like most ships, was a wooden one with three tall masts. Each mast held several huge canvas sails. It took three dozen sailors to raise and lower the sails to catch the wind that pushed the ship through the water. Have you ever been on a ship before?"

"Let me think," I said. "No."

"Well, when a ship moves through the water, the deck tilts slowly, slowly, slowly, to one side, with all the timbers creaking loudly. Then it pauses a moment. Then, slowly, slowly, slowly, it starts tilting and creaking back the other way. This side-to-side motion is called roll. If the waves are high, the front of the ship dips way down and then bucks way up again. This is called pitch."

"Pitch is also a gooey tar used to waterproof boats," I said helpfully.

"Thanks, Missy. I knew that. On the first day of the voyage a storm came up. The wind made waves ten feet high. Now the deck not only rolled and pitched, but it also slid around in a circular motion. This motion I found really annoying. It's called yaw."

"Yaw also happens to be a word in Cattish," I said. "It means Feed me NOW."

"Uh, thanks again. Anyway, most people can't stand the motion of the deck. They get seasick. They lose their sense of balance. They get nausea-causing headaches. They vomit."

"Cats cough up hairballs," I said.

"Uh huh. During this storm, the rolling of the deck got so bad that the boat heeled way over to the side. Huge waves kept washing over the deck. I couldn't walk without falling down. After seven weeks of being tossed about by storms at sea, we finally reached England on Christmas Eve. But guess what? There was no letter from the governor on board—he had never sent it. Governor Keith had lied to me!"

"Well, I don't see why you trusted him. I wouldn't have. So there you were, all alone on Christmas Eve, without any money, in a strange country. What did you do?"

"At first I panicked. Then I relaxed. I realized I could probably find a job as a printer. I did. And London was an exciting place. I happen to love women. I enjoy talking with women as much as men. Probably more than men. I loved the women of London, and the women of London loved me. In London I saw my first concert. And my first play. And I ate in my first fine restaurant—"

"What did you order?" I asked.

"I don't know," he said. "Missy, would you please stop interrupting me?"

"I'm sorry," I said.

"In London the people were polite and sophisticated, like the people in Boston. In London I learned about a new way of thinking called The Enlightenment. The Enlightenment was changing the way people in Europe thought about life. The Enlightenment dared to question things. It questioned the old ways that things had always been done. It questioned the people who had always run things. It questioned the church. The Enlightenment loved science. The Enlightenment loved people who thought for themselves."

"Like me," I said.

"Yes, like you, Missy. The Enlightenment said people weren't stuck in the lives they were born into, as I had been taught. The Enlightenment said that, with serious planning, people could change their lives and become anything they wanted. It was exactly what I had been thinking myself."

"Me, too," I said.

"Good. After almost two years in London, I was homesick. A visiting American businessman offered me a job back in Philadelphia as a printer, and I accepted it. It took the boat two months to get back to Philadelphia. I had time to do some serious thinking. I decided I'd had lots of adventures and fun, but I hadn't done anything I was truly proud of. I was now 20, Missy. I wanted more from life than fun. It was time to pay my debts, to save some money, to put my life in order. It was time to do good things for people. It was time to settle down."

"What happened next?" I asked.

"Nothing," said Ben. "I took the printing job in Philadelphia. I bought The Pennsylvania Gazette. I met you."

"Now the fun begins," I said.

Chapter 5

Ben Gets Married, Starts Philadelphia's First Public Library, First Hospital, First University, First Police Department, First Sanitation Department, First Fire Department, and We Both Start Newspapers (but Mine Is Better)

One day in 1730, Ben woke up, yawned, stretched, and said to me: "Missy, a single man is like half a pair of scissors."

"If that's another aphorism," I said, "I don't get it. Are you saying that a single man can't cut paper? Are you saying that you could stab somebody with a single man? Are you saying that you shouldn't run with a single man in your hand? I mean I just don't get it."

Ben rolled his eyes.

"What I'm saying, Missy, is that I am now 24 years old, and it is high time for me to find a wife."

"Hey, wait a minute. Didn't you tell me just a few months ago that you would never get married?"

"No, that's not anything I would have said."

"You did, Ben. You said it in an interview I did with you. I even printed it in The Philadelphia Feline."

I went to the box where I kept old copies of The Philadelphia Feline and started pawing through them.

"I think you're mistaken," said Ben. "I would never say a thing like that."

I kept pawing through the papers.

"Yes, here it is," I said: 'No ma'am!' Franklin replied. 'I don't ever intend to get married. It would limit me too much. I have too many interests.' There it is, Ben, right on page one! See?"

Ben's face got very red.

"Well, Missy, it seems I changed my mind," he said. "Minds and underwear should be changed every week—otherwise, they start to stink."

"Is that an aphorism?" I asked.

"It is now," he said.

And so, Ben married Deborah Read, the girl who had giggled at him his first day in Philadelphia. Luckily, she liked cats. Debby and I spent many a happy evening, batting a crumpled ball of paper across the living room floor.

Soon after Ben became a complete pair of scissors, Ben and Debby had a son. They named him

William.

It turns out human babies cry all the time. When they're not crying, they're grabbing your tail and trying to stick it in their mouth. Also, they don't know how to poop on the ground and cover it with dirt like the youngest, stupidest kitten in the world, so you have to change their diapers. Outside of the crying, the tail grabbing, and the smell, William was all right.

Ben got a new job. He became official printer for all legal papers published by the colonies of New Jersey, Delaware, and Maryland.

One day Ben asked me a question.

"Missy, why should somebody have to spend a lot of money buying a book every time he wants to read one? Why can't there be a place where people can go to read books for free?"

"Why can't there?" I said.

"I'm going to get 50 of my friends to buy books and donate them to our library. Anyone will be able to come into the library and read the books for free."

"And if they want to take books home with them, they should have to pay a small yearly fee," I said. "The money will go to buy more books."

"Great idea, Missy," said Ben.

"Better fee than free," I said.

"Is that an aphorism?" he asked.

"Sort of. Not really. No."

In 1732 Ben decided to publish an almanac. An almanac is a calendar that contains predictions about the weather a year in advance. It lists the times of future sunrises and sunsets. It lists the times of future high and low tides. It lists holidays and other important dates. Ben's almanac also had recipes, riddles, jokes, and, of course, aphorisms. Ben had me read over the material before we set it in type.

"Ben, here's one I don't get," I said. "'Early to bed and early to rise makes a man healthy, wealthy, and wise.' Are you saying if a sick, poor, stupid man went to bed right after dinner and got up before sunrise, it would cure his sickness and make him rich and smart?"

"Well, maybe not literally, but . . ."

"All right, let me see what else you have. Here's another one. 'Three may keep a secret if two of them are dead.' Oh, now that one I really like."

"Thank you, Missy."

Just as he made up Silence Dogood who supposedly wrote letters to James's newspaper, Ben made up a character who supposedly wrote his almanac—a poor man named Richard Saunders. Poor Richard's Almanack soon became the biggest selling book in the Colonies. Poor Richard's Almanack was translated into many languages and outsold everything but the Bible. It made Ben rich.

"Poor Richard's Almanack is so popular," said Ben, "I've decided to do a new one every year."

"I guess that means you're going to have to come up with a lot more of those annoying aphorisms," I said.

"True."

Now that Ben was rich, he wanted to do things to help the people. He was very concerned about all the sick people in Philadelphia.

Here's how humans treat sickness in the 1700s: Doctors bleed a patient with bleeding cups and leeches—huge, flat, squishy, blood-sucking worms. They prescribe medicines made of ground earthworms, pee, and animal poop. If the patient needs surgery, this is done by barbers, with nothing to kill the pain.

Here's how cats treat sickness in the 1700s: lick it and forget it.

Here's what Ben did for the sick: he helped start Philadelphia's first hospital.

"This city is growing fast, Missy," said Ben, "and people don't feel safe at night. I think they deserve to have some protection." So he also helped start Philadelphia's first police department. "People in this city need a serious place to learn," he said. "A place to study to be scientists, philosophers, lawyers, architects, writers, teachers and doctors."

"Also veterinarians," I said.

"Right. Missy, we need a university." Ben helped start what became Philadelphia's first university.

"The streets in this city are another problem," said Ben. "Because they're made of dirt, when the weather is dry, clouds of dust and sand and dirt hang in the air. The wind blows it into your eyes. It gets into your mouth. It gets into your lungs. It gets into your underwear."

"Cats don't wear underwear," I said.

Ben pressured the city government to pave the streets. Then he got them to start sweeping the streets on a regular basis. Ben had created Philadelphia's first sanitation department.

"Fires are a terrible problem in this city," said Ben. "If a building catches fire now, about all you can do is watch it burn to the ground, along with most of the buildings around it. There are no fire engines or firefighters anywhere in Philadelphia."

So Ben got 30 friends together and formed the first volunteer fire department. Whatever they did for a living, when the fire bell rang, these men met at a firehouse, then raced to put out the fire using leather buckets filled with water. They weren't paid, but they did this to help their neighbors. More volunteer fire departments were formed.

Philadelphia became safer from fires than any city in the Colonies.

In a relatively short period of time, Philadelphia began to change. Because of Ben's inventions, the people of Philadelphia read more, got smarter, became healthier, lived longer, weren't robbed and killed so often, inhaled less dust and did a lot less coughing. The quality of life in Philadelphia got a lot better, and soon other cities in the Colonies began to adopt all of Ben's inventions.

Meanwhile, I had been working hard, writing and printing up The Philadelphia Feline. Many cats bought copies, although few paid with money. Instead I got lots of interesting things in trade—buttons, marbles, feathers, crumpled balls of paper. Letters from satisfied readers began to pour in:

"Dear Editor Hooper: Congratulations! Your newspaper is the finest in the entire history of civilization. Loved your helpful article 'How to Sharpen Your Claws on a Velvet Sofa.' Keep up the good work!
—Horace W."

"Dear Philadelphia Feline: At last, a newspaper for cats who take pride in their cat-hood! Enjoyed the interview with Ben Franklin, but couldn't tell:

is Franklin a cat? If not, why interview him in a newspaper for Feline Americans?
—Puzzled"

"Dear Editor: Thank you so much for creating a newspaper for the intellectual cat. Loved the recipes for Pickled Sparrow Tongues and Chocolate Mouse Foot Surprise. Does anyone there have a good recipe for dried rat tails?
—Shirley M."

In 1732, Ben and Debby had a son they called young Franky. Now there was more crying, more tail-grabbing, and more bad smells. With two young boys in the house getting all the attention, I was starting to feel ignored.

I tried various cute cat tricks to get them to notice me. Like crawling into a drawer or a small box and peeking out. Or sleeping with my paws over my eyes. Or crawling into a paper bag with just my tail sticking out. Here is my favorite cute cat trick. I call it The Tail Problem:

I lie curled up, with one eye open, and notice the tip of my tail is twitching. I act as though the tail has nothing at all to do with me. I act as though the tail is an entirely separate animal. I tense up and pounce on the tail, but it gets away from me. I start chasing the tail, whirling madly around in circles. By now some human has seen this and found it charming. I stop. Then I notice the tail is twitching, and I start the whole process over again.

Debby owned a shop that sold soap, candles, books, sealing wax, pencils, compasses, cloth and chocolate. Ben and Debby seemed to really love each other, but they didn't enjoy the same things. Debby was interested in little else but her family and her store, and she protected both of those fiercely. Like me, Ben was interested in everything and was always out meeting with friends.

I slept in their bed every night, cuddled up between them. They both snored. Loudly.

In 1736 an epidemic of smallpox broke out. Four-year-old Franky caught smallpox and died. Ben and Debby never got over his death.

Chapter 6

Ben Invents a Better Stove, a Better Clock, a Flyless Rocking Chair, Daylight Saving Time, and Nearly Gets Electrocuted by a Kite

"Ben, why is it always cold in our house?" I asked him one day.

"Because, Missy, fireplaces aren't a good way to heat a house. Most of the heat escapes up the chimney and the house remains cold."

So, in 1742 Ben invented an iron stove. It stood in the middle of the room and had a fat pipe to carry smoke outside. It heated rooms better than a fireplace because it kept the heat inside the house.

"When you patent this invention, Ben," I said, "you'll earn a fortune, because then anyone who makes or sells a Franklin stove will have to pay you a special fee."

"I'm not going to patent this stove, Missy. It will be my gift to the cold people of the world."

Ben invented a clock with fewer working parts. It showed seconds as well as minutes.

He invented a set of security mirrors to be

positioned around the front door, so that someone inside could see visitors outside. It was named The Philadelphia Busybody.

He had trouble reaching books on high shelves, so he invented a library chair that turned into a stepladder. He invented a long, mechanical arm—a pole with metal fingers. When you pulled a wire, the metal fingers grabbed the book.

He invented dripless candles.

He invented a chair that fanned him as it rocked, to keep buzzing flies from landing on his bald head.

He invented daylight saving time.

He invented a machine that copied letters.

He invented the first electric battery.

As great as these inventions were, they were nothing compared to the catnip mouse. Sadly, nobody knows who invented the catnip mouse. Here is how to make a catnip mouse:

A human cuts a mouse out of cloth, fills it with catnip and sews it shut. He tosses it to me. I pounce on it and bat it around like crazy until it gets lost underneath the furniture. Folks, it does not get any better than that.

In 1743, a daughter was born to Ben and Debby. They named her Sarah but called her Sally.

In 1748, at the age of 42, Ben retired. He had enough money to make himself and his family comfortable. Now it was time to have some fun. He taught himself French, Italian and Spanish. He pursued his interest in science.

On his daily walks, Ben passed many fields. He noticed that some parts of certain fields were greener than others. He wondered why. He questioned the farmers who owned the fields. He learned that the places where the grass was greenest was where a white powdery mineral called gypsum had accidentally fallen. This led him to invent the first commercial fertilizer.

"Missy, how about this: 'The grass is always greener where the gypsum falls.'"

"That one needs work," I said.

He noticed that plumbers and house painters got mysteriously sick in the same way and was the first to realize the cause of the illness: poisoning from the lead in paint and plumbing pipes.

He studied electricity, which most people did not really understand. He designed experiments to produce small electric charges and give people mild electric shocks. People thought this was a magic trick and they loved it. Ben wanted to prove lightning and electricity were the same, but he didn't know how. In 1752 he designed an experiment to prove it.

He knew that electricity was attracted to metal objects. He wanted to see what would happen if he flew a kite in a thunder storm. He attached a pointed metal rod to the top of a kite. To the bottom of the kite string he tied an iron key. Now all he needed was a storm.

A few days later, on June 10, a thunder storm came. We heard the rumble of thunder and saw flashes of lightning.

"Missy! William!" Ben called. "Get the kite and follow me!"

Ben, William, and I raced to a nearby field as the rain started. William began to run with the kite.

"Tell me when to release the kite, Father," said William.

"Not yet," said Ben.

The rain grew stronger.

"Should I release the kite now, Father?" said William.

"Not yet," said Ben.

The wind whipped at our clothes and almost blew us over.

"Should I release the k-kite now, Father?" said William. His teeth were chattering. His clothes were so wet, they were glued to his body.

"All right, William!" Ben shouted. "Let go of the kite!"

William let go of the kite. It climbed into the storm clouds and disappeared. We waited for something like static electricity to travel down the kite string from the lightning. Nothing happened.

It was pouring rain. Rain was hitting us in sheets. Rain was striking us sideways. We were drenched and cold and miserable. Ben's and William's clothes were so wet they stuck to their bodies. My fur was plastered to my body like a drowned kitten.

"Maybe we should g-go back home!" William yelled over the sound of the rain. "Maybe we should g-give up!"

Then Ben noticed something.

"Missy, look at the kite string," he said. "See how the tiny fibers on the kite string are standing straight out? Just as if they were receiving an electric charge?"

Ben reached out and touched the iron key. We heard a crackling noise. A bright blue spark jumped from the key to his knuckle.

"Yowtch!" he cried.

"Did you get a sh-sh-shock, Father?" William asked.

"Yes!" he shouted. He looked delighted. "It felt like a bite from a small animal! It was the most marvelous feeling! It was an electric shock!"

"C-c-congratulations, Father!" William shouted. "You have proven that lightning and electricity are the s-s-same thing!"

"The shock you got wasn't from lightning!" I shouted. "It was from the electric charge that collected on the wet string from the storm cloud! If that kite had been hit by lightning, it would have electrocuted you!"

Ben laughed uproariously. He had proven that lightning was electricity.

Our kite experiment would become the most famous one of Ben's life. Some people said it didn't happen the way people think. Some said it didn't happen the way he wrote about it in his Pennsylvania Gazette, or that it didn't happen during the summer of 1752, or that it didn't happen at all. Well, I was actually there, and I want to tell you it happened exactly the way I told you.

Also, it led to Ben's most important invention ever.

Chapter 7

Ben Invents the Lightning Rod and Saves Millions of Lives

"Ben," I said one day, "every year houses are struck by lightning, and they burn to the ground. Is there any way we could figure out how to prevent this?"

"An excellent question, Missy," he said. "My guess is that if you attached a pointy metal rod to the top of your house to attract the lightning, and then..." He paused to think.

"And then," I said, "if you attached a wire to the end of that metal..."

Ben nodded excitedly.

"... and ran it down the side of your house into the ground," he said, "then the lightning would follow the wire into the ground without burning down the house. Missy, I think this could work!"

The next day, Ben, William and I climbed up onto the steeply sloping roof of Ben's house. Ben had a long coil of wire over his shoulder. William carried a pointy metal rod. I carried a catnip mouse in my mouth. You never know when you might need a catnip mouse.

"Be very quiet," Ben whispered. "If Debby knew we were up here, she'd be furious."

Just as we got to the chimney, we heard a window being pushed upwards.

"Ben? William? Missy?" called Debby. "Are you up there?"

"Uh-oh," I whispered. "I thought she was in her shop."

"Me, too," whispered Ben. "What are we going to do now?"

"What are you idiots doing on the roof?" Debby shouted. "Do you want to fall off and break every bone in your bodies?"

"Pssst, Ben," I whispered. "Remember that book you were reading yesterday on ventriloquism? Didn't it teach you how to throw your voice and make it seem as if it was coming from somewhere else?"

Ben nodded happily.

"We're not on the roof, Debby!" Ben called. His voice really did sound like it was coming from a different direction. "We're down in the garden! I'm hurt that you thought we were foolish enough to climb on the roof!"

"Well, I'm glad to hear you haven't done that," she

yelled, "but you're certainly foolish enough to do it!" She slammed the window shut. Ben and I burst out laughing.

We began quickly and quietly attaching the metal rod to the chimney, and the wire to the end of the metal rod. As we worked, dark clouds slid across the sky and blotted out the sun.

"Look at that sky," Ben said, tightening the metal rod against the chimney. "We might not have to wait very long to test my lightning rod."

"Those aren't storm clouds, Father," said William.

"I think you're wrong," said Ben. "I think I know a storm cloud when I see one."

"Ben," I said, "I happen to be an expert on storm clouds," I said. "And I agree with William. Those are definitely not storm clouds."

As we began attaching the wire down the side of the house, we heard the first grumblings of thunder.

"If those aren't storm clouds," said Ben, "then what was that noise?"

"That was my stomach grumbling," said William. "I'm hungry for dinner."

By the time we'd gotten the wire all the way down the side of the house and attached it to the foundation, we felt the first few drops of rain.

"And I suppose those drops of moisture we just felt weren't rain," said Ben.

"I didn't feel anything," I said.

"Neither did I," said William.

Just as we stuck the end of the wire into the ground, there was a terrifying explosion of thunder right over our heads. A flash of bright blue electricity snapped and crackled right down the wire into the ground, where it ended with a hiss.

"All right, so I'm not an expert on storm clouds," I said.

In the next issue of Poor Richard's Almanack, Ben told his readers exactly how to make lightning rods for their own houses. Soon lightning rods began appearing all over the Colonies, then all over the world. And letters of thanks poured in from grateful people whose houses and lives were saved by lightning rods.

In Paris, King Louis XVI ordered lightning rods installed on the top of a church steeple. During the next electrical storm, hundreds of Frenchmen stood in the rain and cheered as the lightning rods on the church steeple drew electricity from thunderclouds and sent it snapping and crackling harmlessly into the ground.

Yale, Harvard, Oxford University, the University of St. Andrews, and the College of William and Mary gave Ben honorary degrees. They said he had done more for knowledge than if he'd taken all the courses they offered. He was also honored by the Royal Society of Scientists in London.

Just as he did with his Franklin stove, Ben refused to patent his lightning rod.

"Let's just say it's another gift to humanity, Missy," said Ben.

At age 47, Ben Franklin had become the most famous American in the world.

Chapter 8

I Get My Big Chance to Create History Too

It was a warm summer's day. I was bounding through a field of tall weeds in back of Ben's house, snapping at flies and chasing small furry things just for the fun of it. The bugs were making a high-pitched buzzing sound. Suddenly, a tall gray tiger cat appeared out of nowhere.

"Dowr mee Missy Hooper?" said the cat. Which meant "Are you Missy Hooper?" in Cattish.

I thought he wanted to fight. I flattened my ears, raised my back, and fluffed up my tail.

"Meer browr merff?" I answered in Cattish. Which meant "Who wants to know?"

"My name is Ichabod Pudding," he said, switching to English. "I'm a member of the Feline Historical Society, New England branch. Have you heard of us?"

"No," I said. I unflattened my ears, lowered my back, and unfluffed my tail.

"That's not surprising," he said. "The Feline Historical Society is a secret society. We keep records of the lives of the most famous humans in history. We assign their cats to write about them. Some of our historians have been the cats of Attila the Hun, Ivan the Terrible, Catherine the Great, Erik the Red, Ethelred the Unready . . ."

"What if a famous human has a dog instead of a cat? Do you assign dogs to write their masters' biographies?"

Ichabod Pudding rolled his eyes.

"Please," he said. "I do hope that wasn't a serious question."

"Why?"

"Are you kidding me? A dog could never write his master's biography. A dog could never admit his master was anything but perfect, so he could never write the truth about him. A cat might love his master as much as a dog—or even more—but a cat would always tell the truth."

"I suppose you're right," I said. "So, what can I do for you?"

"Your human, Ben Franklin, is now the most famous American in the world. We at the Feline Historical Society have admired your writing in The Philadelphia Feline. We would very much like you to write his biography for us."

They what? They admired my writing in The Philadelphia Feline? These cats are really nice. And a lot smarter than I thought.

"I would definitely like to write about Ben for the Feline Historical Society," I said.

"Good," said Ichabod Pudding. "We'll expect the first few chapters in a month. Per muffer." Which meant "Good luck."

When I first started writing, I dipped my claws directly into Ben's ink well. After I spilled ink all over his papers a few times, Ben poured ink into a bowl to make it easier for me. In four weeks I had written the first few chapters of his biography. Ichabod Pudding came by our house to look them over.

"So, what do you think?" I said after he had read the manuscript.

"Well, I like all the stories about Ben Franklin," he said. "But I'm not sure we need so much information about your own personal life. About Fluffy, Mrs. Hooper, and all the rest of it."

"Oh, but I'm a huge part of the Franklin story," I said. "Without knowing all about me, the reader will never understand the forces that shaped Ben's life."

"Uh huh," said Ichabod Pudding. "Well, we'll decide later whether to keep it in.

Chapter 9

No Room at the Inn, Then Ben Gets an Idea

In 1753 Ben was named Deputy Postmaster General for the six northern colonies.

At that point it was taking at least six weeks to send a letter from Philadelphia to Boston. Sometimes the letter took several months to get there. Sometimes it didn't get there at all. Ben and I got into his horse-drawn carriage and we took a 10-week tour of the Colonies, from New Jersey to Massachusetts, trying to find out why the mail delivery was so slow. The roads were rutted, the carriage lurched and bounced, and the horse was seldom able to go faster than four miles an hour.

Ben talked face to face with relay riders and postmasters, taking notes on their complaints and suggestions. He mapped out more direct roads to towns, and shortcuts over rivers using bridges and ferries. He devised a series of mile markers to help relay riders pace themselves between destinations—

mile makers that still exist between Boston and New York. All of these improvements would eventually reduce the travel time between Philadelphia and Boston from six weeks to three, then shorten the travel time of a letter between New York and Philadelphia to only one day. That's faster than it is today.

Every night of our trip we stopped at a tavern to eat and sleep. Taverns were a important part of life in the colonies. Most taverns served breakfast, lunch, dinner and drinks. You could dance there, play cards or a form of bowling called ninepins, and you could also sleep there. Taverns held court sessions and public meetings. Business was conducted at taverns between farmers and town merchants. Taverns were centers for people to receive mail, catch up on news, and debate politics.

One night, after riding all day through a freezing drizzle, we stopped at a tavern with a tall brick chimney. Pleasant-smelling wood-smoke billowed from the top of the chimney.

"You know what I'd love now, Missy?" Ben said. "I'd love to sit down beside a crackling fire in the fireplace and eat a steaming hot dinner. I wonder if they have New England clam chowder on the menu here."

"I'm starved too," I said. "I wonder if they have

New England rat chowder."

We went inside but found there was no room left beside the brick fireplace with the crackling fire. More than a dozen customers had taken every available seat.

"Well, so much for sitting next to a crackling fire," I sighed.

"We'll see about that," Ben replied with a twinkle in his eye. He called out to a waiter: "My good man! Please fetch a basket of oysters and bring it to my horse!"

"A basket of oysters for your horse, sir?" the waiter repeated. He looked confused. The other customers turned toward us and stared.

"Yes," said Ben, "but do make sure it's a big basket. My horse is really hungry."

The waiter got a basket, filled it with oysters and walked outside, followed by all the customers, who were dying to see the oyster-eating horse. They returned a few minutes later to find me and Ben sitting alone in a comfy chair right next to the fire.

"Sir," said the waiter, "that horse of yours wouldn't even touch those oysters."

"Well then, my good man," said Ben, "get the horse some hay, and give me the oysters."

In his travels Ben had a chance to visit all the Colonies. He seemed upset by what he saw.

"Missy, each of our colonies is being run as a separate country," he said. "They don't help each other. They have almost nothing to do with each other."

"I noticed that," I said. "What do you suggest?"

"I've written something up. I call it A Plan for a Union of English Colonies in America." It proposes that the colonies help each other with defense and trade. That each colony send a representative to a Great Council led by a president, who would be appointed by King George II."

"I think you're onto something," I said. "If the Colonies could work together, it would solve so many of their problems."

Ben sent a copy of his plan to all the Colonies. He also sent one to King George II.

The colonists didn't like Ben's idea. They thought a president appointed by the king would be too powerful. King George II didn't like Ben's idea either. In fact, he hated it. He thought it would give too much power to the colonists. Although it would take many more years to come about, by writing up this paper Ben had actually invented the United States of America!

Chapter 10

Sailing across the Ocean Is Safer Than, uh, Swimming across the Ocean

At dinner one night in 1757 Ben seemed troubled. Debby asked what was wrong.

"It's that blasted Penn family," said Ben. "They live in London, they own most of the land in Pennsylvania, but they still refuse to pay taxes to the Colony on their land. Even King George II pays taxes on land he owns in the Colonies."

"Well, there's not much you can do about the Penns," said Debby.

"The Assembly thinks there is," said Ben. "They want me to either convince the Penns to pay taxes or else get the British government to give Pennsylvania control of the Penns' land. They've asked me to go to England."

"And you, of course, told them No," said Debby.

"As a matter of fact, I told them Yes," Ben answered quietly.

Debby looked as though she'd been slapped in the

face. Her cheeks got very red. Her eyes shone.

"Surely you don't expect me to come with you to England," she said.

"Yes, I had hoped to take the entire family," said Ben. "You, William, Sally, and Missy."

"Surely, Ben, you remember my intense fear of sailing. Surely you remember my saying that I shall never attempt to travel across any body of water larger than a bathtub. Surely you remember that."

"Debby, traveling by ship is safer than . . . than traveling by horse and carriage. Traveling by ship is safer than walking."

"Safer than walking?" she said. "Are you insane? When you're walking, can you be attacked by pirates? When you're walking, can you be caught in a hurricane and capsize and drown? Ben, if you can find me a footpath across the ocean to walk on, I shall gladly come with you to England. Gladly. Otherwise, I shall stay in Philadelphia."

We knew that Debby was afraid of sailing. Debby knew that in England Ben would insist on going to lots of social gatherings at which she would feel uncomfortable and out of place. More importantly, Debby wanted to keep her family together, and she thought that if she said she was definitely staying in Philadelphia, Ben wouldn't go to England without her.

Debby was wrong. It was decided that Debby would remain at home in Philadelphia with Sally. Ben, William, and I would go to England. Ben promised Debby and Sally we'd be back in just a few months.

Our stay in England would actually last several years. It would also turn Ben from a lover of England into a hater of all things British.

CHAPTER 11

Ben Invents a Musical Instrument, Becomes a Doctor, and Spoils William Rotten

Ben was delighted to return to England. Last time he was in London it had been as a starving 18-year-old. Now he was a rich and famous 51-year-old.

London was dirty, noisy and over-crowded. People in London were either very rich or very poor. Mostly they were very poor, but Ben was rich now, so we saw a lot of the rich. Rich men wore tight knee-length pants called breeches with stockings and buckled shoes. They also wore three-cornered hats and wigs. Rich women wore petticoats under their dresses with wire hoops to make them stand out like big bells. The rich lived in lavish mansions, went to lots of dinner parties and plays and the opera.

Ben rented us four rooms in the center of London in the home of a widow named Mrs. Stevenson. It was in a neighborhood of printer's shops and booksellers. Ben was welcomed by British scientists who admired his electrical experiments and his lightning rod. But when he tried to get the Penns to pay taxes, they angrily refused.

"You own most of the land in Pennsylvania," said Ben, "yet you still refuse to pay taxes to the Colony on your land."

"Correct," said Thomas Penn.

"Even King George II pays taxes on land he owns in the Colonies," said Ben.

"If King George II wishes to pay taxes to the Colonies," said Thomas Penn, "that's his business. We don't do most of the things that King George II does, and that includes paying taxes to the Colonies."

Ben realized this was a complicated mission and it was going to take some time.

William enrolled in a university to study law. I signed up for a class in bird-watching, and two classes in mouse-watching. We settled in for a long stay in London.

"If we're going to get anyone in London to help us against the rich and powerful Penns," said Ben, "we're going to have to make some important friends. And the best place to make friends is at dinner."

Ben bought us memberships in 60 private eating clubs. These fancy clubs didn't seem to mind a cat sitting at the table, so long as I ate neatly from a bowl and had a bib tied around my neck. While

Ben and William dined on English meat pies, Ben introduced me to the delights of goose liver paste and caviar. (Caviar is fish eggs, which is just as yummy as it sounds.) Ben said I was putting on weight. I said he was mistaken. Once I even went so far as to weigh myself. But the British measured weight in something called stone, not pounds, so it was hard for me to tell. (A stone equals 14 pounds, I found out.)

Ben was a fine musician. He played the violin, the harp, and the guitar. One night at dinner Ben heard a man play music by rubbing a wet finger around the rims of thin drinking glasses. Ben loved the sound.

"Ben, why don't you design a musical instrument made out of thin drinking glasses?" I suggested.

We went to a glass blower and Ben ordered several glasses of different sizes. We mounted them side by side on a rotating rod. When Ben played them, the sound was pleasant. Ben called this instrument a glass armonica. The English were charmed by the glass armonica. Composers as famous as Mozart and Beethoven wrote compositions especially for it!

For all his amazing accomplishments, The University of St. Andrews in Scotland awarded Ben an honorary Doctor of Laws degree. Oxford University also gave Ben an honorary doctorate degree. From that point on, Ben was always addressed as Dr. Franklin, even though his only real education had been two years in elementary school.

In 1760, Ben's efforts to tax the Penn family finally paid off: the Pennsylvania Assembly passed a bill taxing the Penns, and the friends Ben had made in the British government approved the Pennsylvania Assembly's action. The Penns were finally forced to pay their taxes. Letters of congratulations to Ben poured in from Pennyslvania.

The Penns were furious with Ben.

"You shouldn't be angry with me," said Ben. "I have helped you become more like King George II. Perhaps someday you'll even have your own castle."

The Penns didn't even crack a smile.

"Well, Ben, we've accomplished our mission in England," I said. "Now we can go back to Philadelphia."

"Yes," said Ben. "Or we could stay here awhile longer. You know, Missy, I am totally happy here. Frankly, I feel so at home in London now, I consider myself almost more English than American."

I was too shocked to answer him. It was true our life in London was very pleasant. It was one continual round of eating clubs, catnip clubs and parties. But I couldn't believe that Ben didn't miss Debby and Sally enough to go back home.

Debby wrote Ben many loving letters, asking

when he was coming home. "How I long to see you," she wrote to him in 1770, five years into his second trip to London. "If you're having the gout that makes your legs and feet swell up so painfully, I wish I was near enough to rub it with a light hand." A few months later she wrote, "When will it be in your power to come home?" and a few months after that she pressed him: "I hope you will not stay longer than this fall."

Ben wrote Debby very few letters, always promising to come home soon—in a few months, after just one more winter, and so on—but he never kept his word. Some people think Ben was having too much fun with all the women in London who hovered over him like honey bees over snapdragons. I do think that's part of the reason, but I think it's also something else, something bigger, something sadder. Ben and Debby's beloved son Franky died of smallpox at age four, because there was a delay before he could be given a smallpox inoculation. Ben secretly blamed himself for this delay, and this guilt poisoned his marriage to Debby.

Ichabod Pudding was right. A dog would never write this about his human, but I will: As much as I loved Ben, I thought he was wrong. Wrong to consider himself an Englishman. Wrong to have spent so many years away from his wife and daughter in Philadelphia. Wrong to have pushed William into friendships with the richest, most snobbish people of London.

Ben was spoiling him rotten. I used to like William. Now I thought he was a snobbish, stuck-up bore. Ben had been trying for years to get William a royal appointment as governor of New Jersey. In 1763, he finally succeeded.

"Well, Missy," Ben proudly announced, "William is now governor of New Jersey and an officer of the British Empire. That's a pretty unusual honor for an American, don't you think?"

"Gracko," I said without much enthusiasm.

Ben frowned.

"Missy, you've been acting so strangely toward William lately," said Ben. "Almost as if you no longer love him."

"Ben," I said, "William is your son. He's our family. So of course I love him. I'm just not sure I like him."

"Well, we're going back to America," said Ben. "After five years it will be good to get back."

"And if William could govern New Jersey from England," I said, "I'm sure he would stay in London."

Ben gave me a dirty look.

Chapter 12

Hello, America. I Must Be Going.

It was 1764. We had been back in Philadelphia for less than two years, but Ben was already itching to return to London. King George III, who had taken over the throne four years ago, was proving he was no friend of the Colonies.

"Debby," Ben announced one night at dinner, "the Pennsylvania Assembly has asked me to go to London again to represent their interests with the King."

"I hope you told them No," said Debby. "You're exhausted, Ben. You've been away from home for five years. I'm just getting to know you again. Please don't leave me now."

"Debby, come with me to England," said Ben.

"Maybe you don't remember who I am, Ben," she said sadly. "I'm the lady who doesn't sail across oceans on ships. Remember? I'm the lady who only goes places she can walk to or ride to in a carriage."

"Debby, with you or without you, I have to go back there," Ben said. "I don't really have a choice."

"Yes, you do, Ben," she said. "You have a choice. If you go to England now, you will never see me again."

"What is that supposed to mean?" he asked.

"Whatever you think it means," she answered.

"Are you threatening me?" he asked.

"No," she said.

"Then what?"

"I just have a very bad feeling about this."

"Debby, I'm not at all excited to leave you again," said Ben. "But I know my country needs me. I must go. I must."

"Fine," she said. "Then go."

"Are you angry at me?"

"No, I'm not angry at you," she said. "I'm not anything at all."

She crossed her arms over her chest and stalked out of the room.

Ben and I returned to London.

Debby was right. Ben would never see her again.

Chapter 13

Parliament Passes Unfair Taxes and Debby Gets Tough with a Mob

In 1765, Parliament passed The Stamp Act. Ben explained it to me:

"The Stamp Act says that from now on, Missy, every printed paper the colonists buy has to have a stamp on it to show they've paid a tax."

"What kind of printed paper do you mean?"

"Marriage licenses, wills, and college diplomas. But also newspapers, books, almanacs, and playing cards."

"That sounds so unfair," I said, "making the colonists buy all those expensive stamps."

"Oh, I don't think they're so expensive," said Ben. "And I don't think the tax is unfair. I think the Colonies won't mind the stamps at all."

He couldn't have been more wrong.

Several weeks later we got a letter from Debby that told us what the Colonies thought about The Stamp Act. They were outraged. They said they hadn't voted on the Stamp Tax, so they weren't going to pay it: "No taxation without representation!" they shouted. There were riots in Boston, Philadelphia, New York, Portsmouth, Charleston, Savannah, Albany, Annapolis, Newport, and New Haven. Mobs attacked tax collectors' homes.

The Penns were still angry that Ben had forced them to pay property taxes in Pennsylvania. They spread a rumor that it was Ben who had created the Stamp Act.

In a letter, Debby wrote to Ben that one night in Philadelphia, an angry mob surrounded the Franklins' house. The mob was loud and carried flaming torches. Debby opened the door and faced the mob. She held a rifle in her hands.

"What do you want?" Debby asked the mob in a strong voice.

The mob was startled and nervous, seeing Debby with a gun. None of them were carrying guns. The reflections of the torches flickered on their faces.

"We're all, uh, pretty angry at Ben about the Stamp Act," said the leader of the mob. "We came here to burn his house down."

"Well, Ben isn't here," said Debby. "Hasn't been for years. He's in England, fighting for the rights of Pennsylvanians. He forced the Penns to pay taxes on their land —maybe you heard? That got the Penns

mad, so they made up a lie that The Stamp Act was Ben's idea. It wasn't Ben's idea. If you want to burn Ben's house down, that's fine with me, but you'll have to go to London, because that's where Ben's house is. I'll even give you his address. But my family lives in this house. If you want to burn it down, that's not fine with me and I need to know about that right now."

Debby cocked her rifle and looked down the

barrel at the mob. The firelight danced on the long barrel of her gun.

"Actually," said the leader of the mob, "now that we've cleared up this silly misunderstanding about The Stamp Act, burning down your house won't be necessary after all."

"Good," said Debby.

"I guess we'll just be going then," said the leader of the mob.

"Fine," said Debby.

"So, uh, nice talking to you," said the leader of the mob.

The mob blew out their torches and shuffled away in embarrassment.

When Ben heard how Debby had handled the mob he wrote her a letter of congratulations. Although Ben certainly hadn't objected to The Stamp Act before, he now saw how much the Colonists hated it. He became a loud opponent of The Stamp Act.

Ben was asked to appear before the British House of Commons to explain the Colonists' reaction to The Stamp Act. Naturally, I went with him.

The House of Commons was part of Parliament, the British government. The House of Commons made the laws and their members were elected by English voters. The other part of the Parliament was the House of Lords. They passed the laws and their members inherited their jobs. Before the War of Independence, America wasn't even a country, it was just a bunch of colonies owned by England. Most people in the colonies had more allegiance to their own colony than to the Colonies as a group.

In the House of Commons Ben was quizzed for four hours about The Stamp Act, but the members of the House of Commons still didn't understand.

"In my opinion," Ben told the House of Commons, "unless you cancel The Stamp Act, the Colonists will refuse to buy any products made in England."

"Surely you jest," said a member of the House of Commons.

"No, actually I'm quite serious," said Ben.

"You're saying they will refuse to buy any products made in England?" the man asked.

"That's right," said Ben.

"What about our lovely English crumpets?" asked another member, a woman.

"I don't know," said Ben, "but probably not."

"What about our lovely scones and quince jellies?" she asked.

"I would assume that if the Americans refused to buy any products made in England," said Ben, "then that would include your lovely scones and quince jellies."

So, Parliament canceled The Stamp Act. Ben became a great hero in America. Three colonies besides Pennsylvania—Massachusetts, New Jersey and Georgia—asked him to represent them in England.

But the British government hadn't learned a thing from The Stamp Act riots. Parliament now placed taxes on glass, paint, paper, lead, and tea. I could not believe how stupid they were! Crowds rioted in Boston and other cities in the Colonies. These protests made Parliament really nervous. The House of Lords called a special session and asked Ben more questions about the Americans.

"Dr. Franklin," said a Lord with a white beard, "it appears that the Colonists are in some sort of a tizzy about those new taxes we thought up. We were kicking around the idea of possibly canceling a few of them."

"I think that would be wise," said Ben. "But why don't you cancel them all?"

"Oh, no, no, no," said the white-bearded Lord, "I hardly think we need go that far. We were thinking of canceling just the tax on lead."

"Just on lead?" said Ben. "Why not all of them?"

"All right then," said the white-bearded Lord, "what about lead and paint? Or lead in paint?"

"In my opinion," said Ben, "I don't think that would really be enough."

"All right," said the white-bearded Lord, "then what about this: lead, paint, paper, and glass? What about canceling the tax on everything but tea?"

"You still want to keep the tax on tea?" said Ben.

"Right," said the white-bearded Lord.

"Well, why not?" said Ben. "What could possibly go wrong with that?"

So Parliament canceled all the new taxes except the one on tea. Guess what happened? The Colonists stopped buying British tea, of course!

Ben and I wrote many articles making fun of the English government. Ben's were published as separate little pamphlets. Mine were published in a newspaper I called The London Feline. King George III was angry, probably angrier with Ben than with me, unless he was a reader of The London Feline, which I doubt. The king felt that Ben was telling the Colonists to commit acts of rebellion against the Crown. The king longed to humiliate Ben. Soon he would have his chance.

Chapter 14

Ben Becomes a Hot-Headed Young Rebel at Age Sixty-Eight

Things were getting ugly in the Colonies between the Colonists and the occupying army of British Redcoats, especially in Boston.

After a snowball attack on a British soldier, a street fight broke out in Boston between a group of Colonists and a few British soldiers.

"The soldiers panicked and fired into the crowd," said Ben. "Unfortunately, they killed five Colonists. Sam Adams called this The Boston Massacre. It was nothing approaching a massacre, but the name seems to have stuck and it has stirred up a lot of anger among the Colonists."

On the evening of December 16, 1773, the next big thing happened in Boston—the Boston Tea Party. It took place in Boston Harbor, which holds so many ships that their masts look like trees in a forest. There were three ships from England—the Dartmouth, the Eleanor, and the Beaver. They were loaded with chests of tea that they hoped to sell to the Colonists, but the Colonists hadn't bought it yet. They were refusing to pay the tax that the British had put on the tea. Sam Adams, a Colonist leader who really didn't like the British, got together about 50 of his friends to protest the tea tax. He shouted, "No taxation without representation!" That meant we refuse to pay the tea tax because we didn't have anybody in England to object when King George decided to put a tax on it.

Sam Adams told them to disguise themselves as Indians so the British wouldn't know who they were, and to sneak on board the three ships and throw all the tea into Boston Harbor. Ben and I were still living in London, so we weren't able to find out exactly what happened during the Boston Tea Party. We needed to talk to somebody who had just taken a ship across the Atlantic from the Colonies.

Then, one night a month after the Boston Tea Party, I heard a scratching at the door. Ben had gone to bed, so I went to the door and opened it.

There, in the doorway, was a very familiar-looking cat. At first, I couldn't remember who he was, but then it hit me. It was Ichabod Pudding from the Feline Historical Society, who'd asked me to write Dr. Franklin's biography.

"Ichabod, I'm so glad to see you!" I said. "What

on earth are you doing here in London?"

"I'm here on business," said Ichabod. "To see how the cats of Thomas Jefferson and John Adams are doing on their biographies. But I wanted to see you too because I was at the Boston Tea Party before I left for England, and I thought it would help you with your Ben Franklin biography if I told you what happened there."

"That would definitely help me," I said.

"Good. Well, I was in the room with a bunch of Colonists when Sam Adams told them to paddle out to the ships and throw all the tea overboard."

"How did you convince them to take you with them?" I asked.

"I didn't," said Ichabod. "It was already dark, and I just followed them down to the rowboats and snuck onboard. By the time they discovered me, it was too late to take me back to shore."

"It was December," I said. "Wasn't it awfully cold out on the water?"

"Cold as an icehouse," said Ichabod. "I was shivering, and my teeth were chattering. The men in my boat said I was making so much noise I'd wake the sailors on the ships.

"When we reached our target ship, the Dartmouth, we tried to keep as quiet as we could, paddling around it in the dark, looking for something we could climb up. All we heard was the slaps of waves on the ship's sides and the creaking of the decks. We finally managed to scramble up an anchor rope. I lost my grip and almost fell into the freezing water. And you know how much cats hate water, even if it's warm."

"I do," I said. "Although tigers are cats, and they love water."

"I knew that," said Ichabod in what I thought was a hurt voice.

"I'm not suggesting you didn't," I said quickly. "Do you have any idea how much tea was dumped into the harbor?"

"Absolutely. When we added up the number of chests of tea from all three ships, it came to 342. By the time the sky grew pink in the east, there were 90,000 pounds of tea leaves floating in the waves. There was a definite smell of tea in the air. Being a cat, I don't like the smell of tea."

"Me either," I said.

"They're now calling what we did that night the Boston Tea Party," said Ichabod. "If that was a party, it was a lot more work than any party I've ever been to."

CHAPTER 15

A Lover of England Turns into a Hater of England within an Hour

Six weeks after the Boston Tea Party, on January 29, 1774, Ben was called before the Privy Council—a group of the king's royal advisors—in Whitehall Palace. As usual, Ben took me with him.

Ben was wearing a brown velvet suit. I was wearing my usual black fur suit with white markings. People in fancy satin clothes and white wigs stared at us when we entered the room in Whitehall Palace where the Privy Council was meeting. We stared back. Nobody asked me to leave, so I took a seat next to Ben.

The Privy Council met in a large courtroom called The Cockpit. This courtroom had a very high ceiling and a huge fireplace, and it was paneled in very dark wood. It looked like a place in which you should hold a funeral. There was a long table at which three dozen Council members were seated. There was a balcony from which an audience of lords and ladies could look down and watch the trial.

Ben didn't know why they had called him in. The King's prosecutor, Lord Wedderburn, began to speak, and it soon became obvious. The King was mad at Ben.

He was mad at Ben for siding with the Colonists on The Stamp Act.

He was mad at Ben for the Boston Tea Party.

He was mad that Ben had gotten hold of secret letters written by Thomas Hutchinson, governor of Massachusetts—letters that made it seem the British were plotting against the colonies. Ben had the letters printed and sent around so all the colonists could read them.

Ben had been invited to the Privy Council just so that Lord Wedderburn could make nasty charges against him and insult him in front of the most important people in England.

Although Ben was now 68 years old, he had to stand for over an hour as Lord Wedderburn attacked him. During Lord Wedderburn's attack, the Council members and the audience in the balcony laughed and hooted and shouted insults at Ben. I couldn't believe how rude and horrible these supposedly civilized Englishmen were!

Lord Wedderburn was small. He had a long, hooked nose that looked like a hawk's beak. He wore a British lawyer's white wig that was so long it reached halfway down his chest and back, and black robes that touched the floor. He pointed at Ben with a long, bony forefinger and pounded the table to emphasize his points.

"I put it to you, sir," shouted Lord Wedderburn, "that you are disloyal to your King and to all of England!"

"Don't answer him, Ben," I whispered.

"I put it to you, sir," shouted Lord Wedderburn, "that you are a liar, a thief, and a traitor! I put it to you, sir, that you are a rascal, a rogue, a scoundrel, a jackanapes, a fopdoodle, a mumblecrust, and a man totally without honor!"

He pounded the table for every name he called Ben.

"Don't act upset, Ben," I whispered. "Don't react to him at all. He's not making any charges you can answer; he's just calling you names."

Ben stood there in his brown velvet suit, silent and motionless, as if his face was made of solid wood, biting his lip to keep from answering, boiling with anger.

I was boiling with anger myself. Wedderburn, you'll pay for what you're doing today, I thought. Your nose will grow six inches for every lie you tell about Ben. Your nose will hang down like the trunk of an elephant. Your nose will grow so long it will scrape the ground as you walk. Your nose will grow so big, you'll have to carry it around in a wheelbarrow. Small children will burst into tears at the sight of your nose. Ladies will scream and faint. Strong men will turn aside and vomit. The only thing keeping me from biting you right now is my fear of getting an infection.

Ben never answered Wedderburn's charges. When Wedderburn was through, Ben quietly put on his hat, motioned to me, and we left.

I will follow you home, Wedderburn, I thought. I will sneak into your bedroom while you are busy hauling your enormous nose out of the wheelbarrow. I will find your underwear drawer and I will put fire ants in your underpants, the kind that bite really hard and don't let go, even after you kill them.

After the trial, Ben was fired as Deputy Postmaster, which was ridiculous because he was the one who had created the Postal Service in the first place and then made it run smoothly. London newspapers called him Old Traitor, Old Double-Face, Old Snake, and The Most Dangerous Man in America. Lord Sandwich, First Lord of the Admiralty and the man who invented putting meat between two slices of bread, called Ben "one of the bitterest enemies England has ever known."

This had been the most humiliating experience of Ben's life. In one hour, he had been transformed from a lover of England to a hater of everything British. King George III and Lord Wedderburn had turned Ben Franklin into The Most Dangerous Man in America.

CHAPTER 16

We Are Sent on a Top-Secret Mission to Save America

Ben was worried. He had sent two letters to Debby in Philadelphia with no answer. That wasn't like her.

Then on February 20, 1775, Ben received a letter from his daughter Sally. He tore it open excitedly, read a bit, then groaned loudly and let it fall from his hands.

"Ben, what is it?" I asked.

"It's Debby," he whispered. "She . . ."

"She what?" I said.

"She had a stroke and . . . died."

He sank into a chair, his eyes teary, shaking his head.

"Oh, Ben, I'm so sorry," I said. I trotted over and rubbed up against his legs.

"Why on earth did we leave her in Philadelphia?" he said.

"Because she refused to get on a ship," I said.

He made a sound like a hiccup, but it was a sob. I had never heard him cry before.

"Why didn't we drag her onto a ship with us, kicking and screaming?" he said.

I don't know," I said.

"Remember what she said when we left, Missy? If you go to England now, you will never see me again. Well, she was right."

He hurried out of the room, and then I heard more sobbing. He was too embarrassed to cry in front of me. He must have loved Debby more than he showed.

After living in London for so many years, we sailed back to America.

Upon our return to Philadelphia, we learned that two weeks before, while we were in the middle of the ocean, the Colonists had battled the British in Massachusetts, at Lexington and Concord. I wasn't there, but a friend of mine named Perkins, a cat at Buckman Tavern in Lexington, told me the whole story. Here's what Perkins told me:

"Missy, British Redcoats had been occupying Boston for seven years, so there had been a lot of bad feeling between them and the Colonists. The

Battle of Lexington and Concord began to take shape just after midnight on April 19, 1775.

"It seems Paul Revere found out the British army had left Boston to capture the Colonists' military supplies in Concord, and he set out to warn them. He crossed the Charles River by rowboat and slipped past the British warship Somerset. In Charlestown he jumped on a horse and rode to Lexington. He stopped at every house along the route to Lexington. 'The British are coming! The British are coming!' he shouted. He also warned a group of Colonial Minutemen led by Captain John Parker."

"And the Minutemen," I said, "were armed citizens?"

"Right," said Perkins, "armed citizens who trained to be ready to fight the British at a minute's notice. Captain Parker and about 80 Minutemen gathered in Buckman Tavern where I spend most of my time, and we waited for the Redcoats to arrive. After most of the night with no sign of British troops, Captain Parker sent out a scout to look around.

"Around 4:15 a.m., the scout galloped back to Buckman Tavern, shouting, "Not only are the British coming, they're almost here! At least 700 of them!"

Captain Parker knew he was outnumbered. He knew no war had been declared yet. So he told his men, 'Gentlemen, stand your ground! Do not fire unless fired upon! But if they mean to have a war, then let it begin here!'

"Just before sunrise, the first group of British Redcoats marched up the street. All 80 Minutemen poured out of Buckman Tavern with their weapons. They just stood there, watching the Redcoats as they marched into view. I myself stayed inside the Tavern, in case I was needed there.

"A British officer galloped toward the Minutemen, waving his sword. 'Lay down your arms!' he shouted at the Minutemen. 'Do not lay down your arms!' yelled Captain Parker at his Minutemen. 'Disperse and go home!' Almost no Minutemen lay down their arms or went home. Both Captain Parker and the British leader ordered their men not to shoot, but a shot was fired anyway."

So that's the story, according to my friend Perkins, who was actually there. The shot that he mentioned was later called The Shot Heard Round the World. Nobody knows who fired that first shot, but more shots were fired, and several Colonists were killed or wounded.

The Battle of Lexington and Concord was the first military battle between the American Colonists and the British. The Colonists didn't want to escalate this battle into a revolution. But, fresh from his humiliation in the Privy Council, Ben had other ideas.

CHAPTER 17

Ben Loses Another Son

Ben and I went to visit his son William in his office. His office was the cleanest one I had ever seen. The leather-bound books on his shelves were arranged according to height rather than subject. The papers on his desk were perfectly lined up in piles so neat it looked like they had been carefully measured and then glued in place. Not a thing was out of place. I wanted to jump up on that desk and knock everything onto the floor. On the wall were framed portraits of the King and other members of the Royal Family.

It had been 12 years since we had last seen William. I couldn't believe the change in him. He looked like an old man with a sore back. He talked like an old man. He walked and stood and sat like an old man. As Ben had grown more rebellious and eager to consider new ideas, William had grown stuffier and more set in his ways.

William was horrified at those who wanted to be independent from England.

"I find such people offensive," said William. "Personally offensive. I cannot comprehend such feelings."

"But you weren't even born in England," said Ben. "You were born in America. You're not an Englishman! You're an American, just like me."

"Perhaps so, Father, but my loyalty is to my King," said William proudly.

"No, William," said Ben with disgust, "your loyalty is to your father. And your father is among those who strongly feel that America doesn't need a king. That America needs to be free of the king. I ask you to join me."

William shook his head.

"I will not join you, Father," said William.

I looked at Ben. He had tears in his eyes.

"Come, Missy," he said. "We are leaving."

We walked outside. Ben was shaking. I couldn't tell if it was anger or sorrow. I guess it was a mixture of both.

"I cannot believe that my son is more loyal to King George III than to his own father," Ben said. "I cannot believe that."

I wanted to say that I wasn't surprised. I wanted to say that I had seen this coming. I figured it would be better to say nothing.

"I feel betrayed," said Ben softly. "William has betrayed me. I no longer have a son!"

Chapter 18

Ben Is Asked to Write the Declaration of Independence and Says, "Thanks, But No Thanks"

Congress asked Ben to write the first draft of the Declaration of Independence, but he turned it down: "I cannot think of a more thankless task than to write to please a large number of people," Ben said. "Let young Jefferson do it, and good luck to him."

Thomas Jefferson wrote the first draft. Ben and John Adams helped revise it.

The signing of the Declaration of Independence took place on July 4, 1776 in a very large room with a very high ceiling. Although the windows were wide open, it was extremely hot in that room, hotter for me than it was for the 56 delegates who signed it, because I was the only one wearing a fur suit.

Maybe Ben, who had invented something to make rooms warm in the winter, could one day invent something to make them cool in the summer. I would have to suggest this to him when we got home.

A horsefly that had flown in through the open windows went bumbling about the room, bumping stupidly into walls and people. Thomas Jefferson tried to brush it away from his perspiring face. John Adams started to say something about it to Robert Morris and the horsefly almost flew into his mouth.

The handwritten parchment Declaration lay on a table with a black tablecloth trimmed in gold, and the delegates signed by dipping feathered quill pens into bottles of black ink.

When the horsefly buzzed angrily past my nose, I snapped at it but missed. It landed on the Declaration and, without thinking, I leapt up onto the table and swatted it. This time I was successful, but the swatted horsefly left a stain on the parchment.

Ben was very upset with me. He pushed me off the table, apologized to those around him, and tried to rub off the stain with the end of a moistened handkerchief. He got most of it, but not all. If you ever manage to see the Declaration up close, look in the lower left corner and you'll see a faint stain—my signature, you might call it.

John Hancock was the first to sign the Declaration of Independence. He made his signature extra large.

"Now King George will be able to read it without

his glasses," he said, smiling. Then his smile faded.

"Let there be no mistake," said Hancock. "We must be unanimous about this. We must all hang together."

"Yes, we must indeed all hang together," said Ben with a twinkle. "Or else we shall all hang separately."

We all laughed, but Ben was serious. If we lost this war, those who signed the Declaration of

Independence would all be hanged as traitors.

As I well knew, England was the most powerful nation on earth, with the most powerful army. America was the youngest nation in the world—Ben said more than half our citizens were 16 years old or younger. The Colonists' army wasn't even an army, it was a bunch of untrained farmers with rifles, and it was already suffering defeats.

As the Declaration of Independence was being signed, a young man rushed into the room. His shirt was unbuttoned, and his face was streaming with perspiration. He seemed out of breath, as if he'd been running.

"British troops are taking Staten Island in New York!" he announced. "They've already taken Boston!"

Those who were signing paused, looked at the young man a moment, then dipped their quills into the ink bottles and went on signing.

Ben's son William tried to get the New Jersey Assembly to agree to a separate peace with England, but the Assembly refused. The Assembly not only refused, but it cut off William's salary and put him in prison. Ben said William was disloyal and refused to help him.

Ben received a letter from France.

"It's from one of my good friends in Paris," Ben told me. "He says the French are eager to help America beat England. As you know, Missy, France was humiliated by the British in the French and Indian War, and they'd love a chance for revenge. My friend says France could be persuaded to give America a lot of help."

"With France as an ally," I said, "America would have a chance. But without France . . ."

". . . America doesn't have a prayer," said Ben.

Congress asked Ben to go to Paris to try and make France our ally.

"I'm 70 years old," said Ben. "I have kidney stones and gout, a disease that makes my legs and feet swell up so painfully that sometimes I can't walk. My scalp has an itchy rash. My teeth ache so badly I can only eat soft foods. I'm in no shape to go anywhere or do anything, much less take on the responsibility of saving my country."

"I'll help you, Ben," I whispered to him. "We'll do it together."

Ben looked at me and smiled.

"I am old and good for nothing," he told Congress. "I fear there is little left of me to be useful. But if you really want me to, I will go."

Whether we liked it or not, the fate of America was now up to us.

Chapter 19

We Set Sail for France—an Old Man, Two Boys and a Cat

A week before our departure for France, Ben invited his family to a farewell dinner at our house in Philadelphia. His daughter Sally arrived with her son Benny, age seven. William's wife Betsy came with her son Temple, age 16. The house was filled with the most marvelous odor of grilled shrimp.

After the meal, as servants began to pour tea and clear away dessert dishes with the remains of cherry cobbler, Ben stood up.

"As you all know," he said, "in seven days' time, Missy and I will be sailing for France. I don't know how long we shall be gone, but it is certain to be a few years at the least. I'm an old man, and I fear I shall be lonely with only an aging pussycat as my companion."

I flashed him a wounded look, but he ignored me. I wondered if there were any leftover shrimp in the kitchen.

"I am therefore going to ask a favor of all of you, a huge favor," Ben said. "I am fully aware of just how huge a favor it is, and I hope that you will not refuse me." He looked around the table at everybody and then continued. "I would like to ask both Sally and Betsy if they could possibly permit me to take Benny and Temple along on my voyage so that I can have at least two members of my family with me in France."

There was a stunned silence. And then the two boys' faces came alive.

"Can I go, Mom?" asked little Benny excitedly. "Can I? Please, please, please, please, please?"

Sally dabbed at her eyes with a handkerchief.

"Well, I don't know, Benny," she said. "Are you willing to leave me and all your friends here and go to an entirely different country, a country where they don't even speak English, maybe for several years?"

Benny hadn't thought of this. He looked at Ben, at Temple, and then back at his mother.

"You could come and visit me every few weeks," said Benny.

Everybody chuckled.

"Benny dear," said his mother, "it takes over a month to sail to England, sometimes several months if the weather is bad, and France is even farther away than England. How could I possibly visit you every few weeks, even if we could afford it?"

Benny shrugged.

"Are you sure you want to do this, Benny?" his mother asked.

Little Benny nodded his head excitedly up and down several times.

"Well then," said Sally, sighing. "Then I suppose it's all right with me."

Benny shrieked and threw his arms around his mother. She hugged him tight and dabbed at her eyes again with her handkerchief.

Ben turned to Betsy.

"What about you, Betsy?" he asked. "Are you willing to let Temple come to France with me if he's agreeable?"

"Do you realize what you're asking of me?" she asked softly.

Ben nodded.

"I do indeed, my dear."

Ben turned to Temple.

"I would like you to be my assistant in France," he said. "What's your feeling on this, Temple?"

Temple looked at his mother.

"If Mom doesn't mind," said Temple carefully, looking at Betsy, "I think it would be a wonderful opportunity for me to be Grandpa's assistant in France."

Betsy picked up her cup, sipped her tea, burned her tongue and put her cup back in its saucer.

"How can I possibly say yes to such a request?" Betsy asked, looking away from both Ben and Temple. She took a deep breath and then slowly let her lungs collapse, like an abandoned bagpipe. "On the other hand," she said, "how can I possibly say no?"

Before leaving Philadelphia, Ben went to his bank and withdrew several thousand dollars from his personal account and gave it to Congress to help fight the war.

Late at night on October 29, 1776, Ben, little Benny, Temple and I slipped quietly out of Ben's house. We were on a top-secret mission for our country. Neither of the boys had been allowed to tell his friends where we were going or why. A horse and carriage waited for us in the darkness. Little Benny started to speak, but Ben shooshed him. We climbed into the carriage. The driver clucked to the horses and we took off. A clatter of hooves on cobblestones was the only sound in the night.

"Grandpa, where are we going?" asked Benny in a frightened whisper.

"It's a secret," said Ben, "so you can't repeat this. We're going to a ship on the Delaware River called The Reprisal."

"Why is our trip such a secret?" Benny asked.

"Because we don't want the British to know what we're doing," said Ben.

"Why don't we want the British to know what we're doing?" Benny asked.

"Because they might try to stop us," said Ben.

"Why might they try to stop us?" asked Benny.

"Why must you ask so many stupid questions?" asked Temple.

"Why must you?" asked Benny.

"Boys!" Ben scolded.

The carriage pulled up at the dock. We got out. The driver helped us unload our baggage. There was a stiff breeze off the water. You could smell the salt of the ocean, the chilly promise of the coming winter. The Reprisal bobbed quietly at anchor. It was an American warship and it had 16 large cannons mounted on board.

"Grandpa, why are there so many guns on our ship?" Benny asked.

"Because we're at war, Benny," Ben answered. "If we meet up with any British warships, we have to be able to defend ourselves."

The many ropes running up the ship from the

deck to the mast groaned as the ship rode the gentle swells of the water. We heard the soft slap of the waves against the hull. Ben, Benny, Temple, and I were led aboard The Reprisal.

"Do the other people traveling with us know we're on a secret mission?" Benny whispered.

"Nobody else is traveling with us," said Ben.

Benny's eyes got very big.

"You mean we have our own private warship taking us to France?"

"That's right," said Ben.

Benny couldn't believe it.

"That is so amazing!" said Benny. "When can I tell my friends about this?"

"Never," said Temple.

"Grandpa, Temple says I can't tell my friends we have our own private warship to take us to France!"

"Temple is right," said Ben. "This is a secret mission. We can't talk to anybody about it. Not ever."

"The most exciting thing I've ever done in my whole entire life, and I can't tell anybody?" Benny pouted. "That isn't fair!"

The Reprisal cast off and we pulled away from the dock.

"What if the British capture us?" Benny asked.

Ben laughed darkly.

"If the British capture us, I shall be hanged as a traitor," he said.

The boys were both scared.

"If they capture us," Benny asked, "what will happen to me and Temple and Missy? Will they hang us too?"

"Oh, most definitely," said Ben with a wink. "The British are particularly nasty to traitorous boys and pussycats."

The voyage was hard, the seas were rough, and the food stank.

At dinner the first night, the boat rocked slowly back and forth in the swells, the overhead timbers creaking. We sat below deck in the dining area. A crew man put tin plates in front of us with a hunk of something dried and brown on each one. Everyone looked at his own plate, not sure what the brown thing was.

Ben was the bravest. He took a fork and a knife and began sawing away at the brown thing. When he was finally able to detach a piece of it, he popped it into his mouth.

"Pyew!" he said. "What the devil is this?"

"Dried salted beef, sir," said a crewman.

"Really?" said Ben. "It's like gnawing on an old shoe, but not nearly as tasty."

Ben had a skin condition. The salted beef made

his skin a lot worse.

We were at sea for a month. On the morning of November 27, a ship was sighted. An Irish ship. Our captain was an experienced naval officer. He pursued the Irish ship, caught up with it, and commanded it to stop. He and a small party of his sailors armed with muskets got into a small boat, boarded the Irish ship, and captured it without a struggle.

Benny couldn't stop talking about it.

"We captured an enemy warship!" said Benny. "I can't believe we did that!"

"It's not exactly an enemy warship," Ben corrected him. "It's a boat from Ireland and it wasn't armed."

"But Ireland is part of the British Empire," said Benny. "And we're at war with the British. It is definitely an enemy warship and we captured it!"

Benny was even more thrilled when, later that same day, our ship captured another British ship, also without a fight.

"I can't believe we captured two entire ships in a single day!" said Benny. "Let's go out and capture some more! We could probably capture the whole British fleet by ourselves if we wanted to!"

Chapter 20

We Arrive in France and Begin Our Mission

On December 4, we landed in France. Ben was so weak he could stand only if he leaned on a cane. The carriage that would take us to the town of Nantes pulled up. It was a rickety old carriage and it was pulled by a tired old swaybacked horse. "That horse and carriage look the way I feel," said Ben. "We're a perfect match."

We got into the carriage and it set off for Nantes. We traveled for a while, and then the winding road led into a dark forest. At the edge of the forest, the old French driver stopped the carriage to speak to us.

"Just two weeks ago," he confided, "a gang of 18 robbaires keels travelers like you on thees very spot."

"H-how did they kill them?" asked Benny. His voice was higher than usual, and his eyes had grown very large.

The driver shrugged.

"Een ze usual manner," he said. "Ze knifes, ze guns. You know. Ze usual manner."

"D-do they kill you if you give them your money?" Benny asked. His eyes darted here and there, searching the trees and bushes.

"Of course zey do," said the driver. "Zey are robbaires, no?"

"Do they ever kill kids?"

"They prefer to kill kids," said Temple with an evil smile. "Especially little boys. Then you know what they do? They boil them in a big pot and they eat them."

"They do not!" said Benny.

"Do too," said Temple.

"Do not!" said Benny.

"Do too. Ask the driver," said Temple, giving the driver a wink.

"All right, Temple," said Ben. "That will be quite enough."

Luckily, we got to Nantes without meeting any "robbaires." Ben rested a few days, and then we went on to Paris.

In Paris they had learned of Ben's arrival. Wherever we went, crowds gathered to look at him and yell "Bonjour!", which meant hello. Ben was famous for his aphorisms and good advice in Poor Richard's Almanack. His lightning rods were protecting their homes. His Franklin stoves were keeping them warm in winter. They loved him!

Ben was amazed at his fame, but embarrassed because he wasn't looking or feeling his best. Usually he dressed in the latest fashion. In France now, the latest fashion for men was fancy suits of silk or satin with lace cuffs. Both men and women wore white powdered wigs. They wore wigs to hide the fact that they shaved their heads to get rid of lice.

Instead of a satin suit and a wig, Ben was dressed in the clothes he wore on the boat—a plain brown cloth coat, and a big fur cap. The fur cap was my idea—it hid the sores on his head.

The French didn't make fun of Ben's appearance; they loved it. They saw Ben as the Natural Man from America. They saw him as The Frontiersman.

"The Frontiersman? Me?" said Ben. "Missy, this is hilarious. I have never lived anywhere near the frontier. I have only lived in cities and dressed in fancy suits."

"Then from now on you must always dress as the Natural Man from America," I said.

"I couldn't agree more," he said.

"Should I carry a musket?" he asked.

"No," I said, "the fur hat pretty much does the trick."

The French loved Ben's look so much they

tried to copy it. Some ladies even had wigs made in the shape of Ben's fur hat. They began selling tiny painted pictures of Ben on the streets. French ladies wore tiny portraits of Ben in their rings and bracelets. Ben wrote his daughter Sally: "Your father's face is now as well-known as the man in the moon."

A rich French merchant named Chaumont (pronounced Show-MOAN), who loved America and hated England, offered us a huge house to stay in. The house was in a suburb of Paris called Passy (Pa-SEE). Passy was a mile from Paris, seven miles from the royal palace of Versailles (Vare-SIGH), and it had wonderful gardens. Ben accepted. He put Benny in school and Temple became one of his assistants.

The great display of love from the French had a healing effect on Ben. When we first got to France, he was so sick he could barely stand. Now his energy returned, and he was his old self. Ben went to work, trying to figure out how to get the French to be our allies. I went to work, writing a newspaper I called The Passy Pussy.

The people of France were either very rich or very poor. The streets of Paris were open toilets. Street beggars were dying of hunger. But in the court of King Louis XVI the rich threw endless parties. Ben knew that much business was done at dinner parties. He pretended to be just a famous American tourist, going to parties and having fun, but in fact he was a man on a desperate secret mission.

Ben believed France was the most civilized country on earth. I had to agree. The people we met seemed to be better educated and more interested in music and art than the American colonists. The dinner parties we went to served rich French food with lots of buttery sauces and whipped cream. I happen to love buttery sauces and whipped cream. I also love caviar and goose liver paste. We both gained weight. Ben charmed everyone, especially the ladies. If you want my opinion, I thought he overdid it with the ladies.

He was a 70-year-old bald man, so sick he sometimes had trouble standing up. Unlike the ladies we met in Philadelphia, the French ladies surrounded Ben at parties, flirting, giggling, and insisting he kiss their necks. Why did they do this? Probably because, unlike other men, Ben clearly loved talking to women and listening to what they had to say.

He loved playing party tricks. Whenever we were at a party where there was an outdoor pond, he waved his cane over wavy water and it became smooth. Ben's magic trick was based on a scientific fact he'd discovered—oil smooths rough water. His cane had a hollow space to store oil. As he waved his cane over the water, he opened the space that held the oil, allowing a few drops to hit the water.

"Tell me, Ben, how are you planning to get the French to be our allies?" I asked.

"I don't know," he said. "I suppose I'll just make it up as I go along, as I did in England. You know how I love playing chess, Missy. I think I'll play with the

French like they were pieces in a game of chess."

We had heard rumors that the King of France liked both Ben and the Colonists. Ben contacted the French court through King Louis' minister, the Count of Vergennes (Ver-ZHEN).

Our first meeting with the Count of Vergennes took place in an elegant chamber with a very high ceiling. At one end of the chamber was the largest desk I had ever seen. Its legs were carved to look like four tiny ladies who were holding up the desk top. They were painted gold with real gold paint. The desk was so long that if I started running at one end of it and skidded, I could have knocked a huge stack of papers at the other end onto the floor.

As soon as we were seated on the cushions of a long couch, servants brought Ben tea in a tiny teapot decorated with blue and white flowers.

Vergennes was dressed in a satin suit with lace ruffles and a powdered wig. Shortly after the meeting started, he told Ben he was willing to secretly loan the Colonists large amounts of money for weapons and other supplies.

"Count Vergennes," said Ben, "we are deeply grateful to you for your generous help . . ."

"You are more zan welcome," said Vergennes.

". . . but," Ben continued, "if you want to know what would help our brave Colonists even more, it would be to have you send French troops—openly—to join our armies. That would make the American Revolution look like a real war of independence that was supported by other nations, instead of a revolt by a bunch of ragged lunatics."

Vergennes just smiled and shook his head.

"I must be completely honest weeth you, Monsieur Fronklin," said Vergennes. "I am sorry to tell you thees, but we do not theenk zat ze Colonists can beat ze British. And eet would be humiliating to join a losing army, yes? But eef ze Colonists start weening, well, zat would be a different story—zen France would join ze Colonists openly and send zem troops."

Ben nodded, thanked Vergennes, and then we left his office.

"Let me see if I understand this, Ben," I said. "We can only win if we get France to join us, but France will only join us if we're winning?"

"You've got it," Ben replied.

"But that's an impossible situation," I said.

"To turn 'Impossible' into 'Possible,' just remove the first two letters," said Ben.

"I hope that's not another aphorism," I said. "Because if it is, it stinks."

"Hmm," Ben sighed. "You're probably right."

Chapter 21

I Take a Dangerous Midnight Ride to Prove Somebody's a Spy

Too many buttery sauces and too much caviar and goose liver paste. Both Ben and I had put on a lot of weight. I carried it well. With all my fur you could barely tell I'd put on any weight at all. But Ben now had a big fat belly. He hated when I teased him about it.

The British knew that Ben was in France on secret American business, but they didn't know what it was. Secret agents were sent to spy on him.

"I know I'm surrounded by spies," Ben told me. "My own butler is probably a spy, but I wouldn't fire him if he is. Not if he's a good butler."

I didn't think Ben's butler was a spy, but I wasn't so sure about his personal secretary, Edward Bancroft. Ben really liked Bancroft because he was an amateur scientist. But there was something about Bancroft I didn't trust.

One Tuesday night as Ben sat writing a long letter

home to Sally, I lay down on it and tried to get Ben's attention.

"Missy, will you kindly get off my letter?" Ben asked me.

"I will," I said. "But first I want to talk to you about something important."

"If it's about making you a new catnip mouse," he said, "I've already cut out the pattern. All I have left to do is fill it with catnip and sew it shut."

"This isn't about catnip mice," I answered. "It's about spies."

Ben sighed. "Whom do you suspect now?"

"I'm very suspicious of Edward Bancroft."

"Oh, for heaven's sake!" Ben shouted. "Edward is not only a devoted secretary, he's a close friend. He is the absolute last person I would ever suspect of being a spy."

"Then that's one of the best reasons to suspect him," I answered. "There is something about him I just don't trust."

"Nonsense," said Ben. "Sheer poppycock. Forget about it, Missy."

He pushed me off his letter.

"All right," I said, "then I'll investigate him myself. But in the meantime, could you please not show Edward any really secret matters?"

"Missy, the man is my secretary. He sees

everything I do. Now will you please let me write my letter?"

Ben was a wonderful man, but sometimes he just wasn't smart. All right, I wouldn't mention Edward Bancroft again. But I would do my own investigation of him. Cats are better at spying than humans anyway.

Late that night I crept past Bancroft's rooms. It was after midnight. A candle was burning in the window of Bancroft's bedroom. I leapt quietly onto his window sill and sneaked a peek inside.

Bancroft was sitting at a low wooden desk. On the desk beside the candle were an ink well and a sheet of paper. By the light of the candle Bancroft seemed to be writing a letter. I could see that most of the paper was already covered in writing. I didn't know why, but there was something strange about what he was doing.

I looked closer. Now I knew what it was. Bancroft dipped his quill pen into his ink well and then he wrote, but no words were coming off the end of his pen.

How could this be? There were words already on the paper, but none coming off the end of his pen.

Bancroft finished writing. He blew on the letter to dry the ink. Then he folded it twice and sealed it with special sealing wax. He stood up and lifted his long overcoat off a peg on the wall. He put on his overcoat and tucked the letter into his pocket. He walked out of the room.

A moment later Bancroft left his house. He looked around nervously. Then he walked quickly to the back of the house, to the stables. In the stables were the horses that were used to pull the carriages that Ben and the others used to go to Paris.

I followed and watched from the shadows. I'm a mostly black cat, and mostly black cats are invisible in the shadows.

Bancroft whispered to one of our drivers. The driver nodded. The driver must have been a British spy, like Bancroft!

A moment later, the driver took a horse out of the stable and hitched him up to a carriage. Where was Bancroft going at this hour of the night? I had to know. I decided to follow him.

As the carriage began to move, I leapt lightly onto the back of it and crawled up to the roof. The horse picked up speed. The wind ruffled my fur. I hung on tightly with my claws as the carriage moved out of the driveway and onto the main road to Paris.

I had no idea why Bancroft was sneaking off to Paris in the middle of the night, but I was more convinced than ever that he was a spy. And then I had an uncomfortable thought:

Bancroft knew I was a cat who talked. If he was really a spy, he'd do anything to keep from being found out. Perhaps even kill! Had he seen me jump onto the back of the carriage? Had he heard my claws scratching around on the roof as I tried to keep my balance? Did he know I suspected him? Did he know I was now gathering evidence to take back to Ben, evidence that might get Bancroft arrested or even hanged?

Was he, even now, slowly opening the carriage door and sneaking up behind me, ready to pounce like a cat on a mouse and silence my little cat lips forever?

I looked quickly in back of me, but there was nobody on the carriage roof but me. Perhaps Bancroft hadn't seen me after all.

Or perhaps he'd seen me, and he was just waiting for a better time to kill me! And what could be a better time than after midnight on a deserted road to Paris?

When we got to Paris, the city was asleep. The carriage slowed. The horse clop-clopped along the quiet Paris streets till it got to a large park. I recognized the park. It was called the Tuileries (TWEE-luh-rees) Gardens. Why were we going to the Tuileries at this hour of the night?

The carriage entered the Tuileries. The shadows

cast by the trees swaying in the wind were ghostly. Lucky for me, cats don't believe in ghosts. Bancroft signaled the driver. The carriage stopped. Bancroft got out. He looked anxiously in all directions. Then he walked up to a large tree. He reached into his overcoat pocket, pulled out his letter and shoved it into a hole in the tree trunk. The letter disappeared.

Bancroft walked to the carriage and got back inside. The carriage began to move forward. Why had Bancroft put his letter inside the tree trunk? Maybe another spy was going to pick it up from there. Of course! I had to get that letter before it was picked up.

I leapt off the roof of the moving carriage. When cats jump we always land on our feet. I landed hard on the gravel road. My paws stung from the landing. I walked quickly to the tree trunk. I climbed up as far as the hole and looked inside. I could just see the letter. I reached my paw through the hole in the tree trunk and tried to snag it with my claws.

On the third try, my claws caught the edge of the letter and I pulled it carefully out of the tree trunk. Holding the letter in my mouth, I raced off after the carriage. It was too late. The carriage was too far down the road. I would have to walk all the way back to Passy.

By the time I got back to Passy, it was almost light

out. When I slipped into the bedroom of our house, Ben was lying on his back, snoring.

"Ben, wake up!" I whispered. "I have something really interesting to show you!"

Ben went on snoring. His fat belly rose and fell with every snore.

"Ben!" I said a little louder. "You must wake up!"

Ben went on snoring. It sounded like the snuffling and grunting of sows.

I smacked him on the face with my paw, but he didn't even feel it. I walked to the end of the bed. I took a running leap and landed on his fat belly with all four paws.

"Whuff!" said Ben, waking suddenly. "What on earth . . . ? Missy, you wretched cat! What are you doing?"

"Trying to wake you," I said. "I've just returned from Paris. I have something terribly important to show you."

"You've been to Paris? Tonight? Whatever for?"

I dropped the letter on his bed.

"This," I said. "Please open it at once."

"Where did you get this?"

"It's a letter that Bancroft wrote. He took the carriage to Paris after midnight and hid the letter in a hole in a tree in the Tuileries. I think it will prove to you that he's a British spy."

"A spy! Missy, I cannot believe you woke me up just to tell me this poppycock about Edward. What time is it anyway? It must be the middle of the . . ."

Ben reached for his pocket watch. He snapped it open and uttered an angry cry.

"Do you realize it's only five in the morning, you miserable cat?"

"Early to bed and early to rise makes a man healthy, wealthy and—"

"Not funny, Missy!"

"Ben, please. Just read the letter!"

I gave him the letter. Cursing, he lit a candle, broke the wax seal on the letter, opened it and began to read.

"Hmm," he said. "Missy, do you know what this is? A love letter. Poor old Bancroft was just writing a love letter to his girlfriend in Paris. You've stolen it out of the hollow tree, and now she won't get it. I think you owe this man an apology."

Ben got back in bed, turned his back on me, and composed himself for sleep.

I felt awful. I had misjudged poor Bancroft. He wasn't a spy after all! He was Ben's devoted secretary and loyal friend and I had stolen his love letter out of that tree in the Tuileries, and now his girlfriend would think he didn't love her anymore. They would break up, they would both be miserable, they would live alone for the rest of their lives and never marry, and it would all be my fault!

And then I remembered something.

"Ben, listen to this. I watched Bancroft as he finished writing this letter. He dipped his pen in the ink well, but when he wrote on the paper, no words came off the end of his pen."

Ben turned around in bed and looked at me. "What did you say?"

"Bancroft dipped his pen in the ink well, but no words came off the end of it."

Ben's mouth dropped open. His eyes got wide. "Give me that letter again," he said.

I handed him the letter. He got out of bed. He held the letter over the candle, careful not to let it catch fire. I crept closer to watch. The heat from the candle was gradually making more writing appear in the empty spaces on the letter.

"Invisible ink!" I cried.

"Yes," said Ben, "invisible ink. Listen to what is written here: 'Franklin now without a doubt here in France to try and get an alliance with the French. He tries to make connection with King Louis through his minister, the Count of Vergennes . . .'"

"Did I tell you Bancroft is a spy or didn't I?" I shouted.

"Sssshhh!" Ben put his hand over my mouth.

I was going to bite him, but then I decided not to.

"Missy, I owe you an apology. Can you ever forgive me for doubting you?"

"I don't know," I said. "Probably not."

Chapter 22

We Pass Information to Spies

Ben still hadn't made much progress in getting France as an ally. Congress was pestering him to get the French to commit. Ben knew that the Americans were not winning the war enough for France to back them openly and he was careful not to pressure Vergennes for what he knew Vergennes couldn't give him yet.

"Ben," I said. "Edward Bancroft is still working here. You haven't fired him."

"You noticed that, have you?"

"But he's a British spy, Ben. You admitted that yourself."

"Of course he's a British spy, Missy. And if I fire him, the British will just replace him with another spy, and I won't know who it is. But if I keep Bancroft, I know he's the spy, and I can feed him false information."

"What kind of false information could you feed

him?"

Ben chuckled.

"I have already 'accidentally' leaked some information about my evil inventions," he said. "Like that series of giant mirrors I designed? The ones the French are even now in the process of setting up on the cliffs of Calais? To focus the sun's rays on the English Channel and burn up the entire British fleet?"

"Ah yes, the series of giant mirrors," I said, giggling.

"I also leaked information to Bancroft about the electrical machine I invented that will link Calais to Dover, with wires circling the British Isles. The machine that will carry a shock powerful enough to blow the entire British Empire out of the sea!"

"Too bad you let the cat out of the bag on that one," I said.

"A cat in the bag catches no mice," he replied with a wink.

CHAPTER 23

We Push France into an Alliance with the Colonies

December 4, 1777. A bitterly cold day. The wind stung your face, unless it was covered with fur. Yesterday a courier arrived with mail from the latest ship to dock at Le Havre. Among the letters was one from his daughter Sally. Ben started reading the letter aloud to us before he knew what it said.

"Dear Father," Ben began in a cheery voice, "hope that things are going well for you there in France. Here things could be better. The colony of New York has been captured by the Redcoats . . ."

Ben paused a moment, then continued in a quieter voice that was not so cheery: "Six of Washington's battalions were forced to surrender to the British and General Burgoyne's army of 8,000 men has come down from Canada, conquered Fort Ticonderoga, and is now headed south. We have heard rumors that General Howe's army has captured Philadelphia."

Ben stopped, swallowed hard, and continued: "I

am sorry to tell you that British soldiers are living in your house and sleeping in your beds."

Ben put down the letter and stared into space for a moment.

"Sally," he whispered. "May God protect you and the rest of our family."

Ben went to his room and lay down on his bed, staring up at the ceiling. There were tears in his eyes, as if he had been grating onions. I jumped up on the bed and rubbed my head against his hand. He scratched my back in an absent-minded way, worried sick about Sally and the others and unable to do anything at all.

There is no way to get news from the Colonies except by boat and courier, and that takes more than a month in each direction. By now things could be even worse back home and we would have no way of knowing. However, a courier was even now on his way to Passy by horseback to tell us the latest news about the war. He was due to arrive here sometime after dark tonight, unless there was a blizzard.

The day passed slowly. Ben met for several hours with his American assistants, Silas Deane and Arthur Lee, I'm not sure about what. Shortly after dinner we heard a horse gallop up to the house and stop.

The courier!

Without even pulling on a coat, Ben rushed

outside to meet him. The messenger's horse was breathing hard from the gallop and it was covered with sweat. Steam was rising from its wet body and from its nostrils.

"Sir," Ben called out, "Do the British still occupy Philadelphia?"

"They do indeed, Dr. Franklin," answered the messenger.

Ben's shoulders sagged. He turned back toward the house.

"But sir," the messenger continued, "I have greater news than that—America has won a major victory at Saratoga, New York!"

"What?" said Ben.

"We have captured General Burgoyne and his entire army of 7,000 men!"

Ben screamed. I yowled. It was the first major defeat of the British in the war, and it showed that a raggedy band of Colonists could defeat the experienced British forces.

"How did we manage that? Do you know the details?" Ben asked.

It was freezing out and Ben hadn't taken a coat, but he couldn't stand not knowing the details.

"Well, sir," said the messenger, patting his horse's sweating flank, "from what they tell me, it had been Burgoyne's mission to take control of the whole

Hudson Valley, which would cripple the Colonists' army and bring the war to an end . . ."

"Go on," said Ben. His teeth were chattering now from the cold, but he wouldn't go inside until he'd heard the whole story.

"But Burgoyne's victory depended on help from two other British armies . . ." said the messenger.

"One led by General Howe and one by Colonel St. Leger?" said Ben.

"Right, sir," said the messenger. "But instead of helping Burgoyne, for some reason Howe decided to take his troops to capture Philadelphia, and St. Leger's army never arrived. Burgoyne thought he didn't need either Howe or St. Leger. Well, sir, he soon found his army surrounded and outnumbered. Burgoyne was forced to surrender!"

Ben gave a little victory yelp, thanked the messenger and shook his hand. Then we raced back inside the house where it was warm to tell Silas Deane and Arthur Lee.

"This is wonderful news, gentlemen," Ben said. "This turns the whole war on its head. Now, suddenly, the Colonists are winning!"

We celebrated that night. So did all of America's friends in France.

Vergennes said that because of Burgoyne's surrender, France might now be ready to consider an alliance with the Colonies. Ben, Silas Deane, and Arthur Lee wrote up a list of our conditions for an alliance with France. Vergennes took the list to King Louis XVI.

Bancroft and the other British spies immediately reported this to London. The possibility that France would now become an ally of the Colonists scared the pants off England.

The British sent a representative to Ben to talk about a possible cease-fire. I slipped into the sunny room in our house where they were meeting and drinking tea.

"Under what terms might England consider stopping the war?" Ben asked the British representative.

"King George wants peace at any price," said the British representative, leaning back in his chair, his legs crossed, sipping tea from a delicate blue and white china cup.

Peace at any price? I couldn't believe my ears. This was very good news indeed!

I hopped onto the back of Ben's chair, right up near the side of his head. The sun shining in through the window warmed my fur.

"Is the King willing to grant the Colonies independence?" Ben asked.

"Independence?" spluttered the British

representative, spitting tea all over himself. "Oh my, no! Good heavens, no!"

"I thought you said the King wants peace at any price," said Ben.

"Almost any price, my good man," answered the British agent, dabbing with his handkerchief at the spilled tea on his moustache and on the front of his shirt. "Almost any price."

Very soon after that, the British agent stood up, thanked Ben for the tea, made his goodbyes, and left.

"What was that all about?" I asked. "I thought he was coming here to make a deal."

"So did I," said Ben.

"Why did he even bother coming here?" I asked.

"I'm not sure, Missy," said Ben, "but I had hoped for something quite a bit better than this. Now we're really in a fine fix. Time is running out on the Colonists. Our armies need help desperately. We're out of guns. We're out of ammunition. We're out of food. We're out of money."

"I know," I said.

"I've been playing elaborate games with the Count of Vergennes for a long time. Trying to get him to say that France will formally recognize the Colonies as a nation. Trying to get the French to lend us more and more money. Trying to get him to give us some troops. Pressuring him as much as I dared, but knowing it isn't up to Vergennes, it's up to King Louis XVI. Vergennes has been stalling me for weeks."

He sighed.

"I'm worried now that if French help comes at all, it will come too late," he said.

"What will you do if it comes too late?" I asked. "Try to make peace with the British at any price?"

Ben thought a moment, then shook his head.

"No," he said. "Certainly not at any price. But what I must do now is make Vergennes believe I'm seriously considering a British peace proposal. The last thing France wants at this point is for America to sign a peace treaty with the British."

Ben made an appointment to see the Count of Vergennes. When the day of the meeting arrived, Ben deliberately arranged for us to leave our house a half hour late. By the time we arrived in his office, Vergennes was almost jumping out of his skin.

"So, Monsieur Fronklin," said Vergennes, after we had been seated on soft cushions and a servant had brought Ben a steaming cup of tea and me a bowl of warm milk, "I have heard a rumor zat ze British have offered you ze proposal of peace."

"Oh," said Ben with a thin smile, "is that what you heard?"

"Yes," said Vergennes.

"Then perhaps it is true," said Ben.

Vergennes looked like he was ready to have a litter of kittens.

"What can we do to stop ze Colonies from accepting a proposal of peace from ze British?" he blurted.

"France must formally recognize America as a nation," said Ben.

I jumped onto the back of Ben's chair and stretched my paws out in front of me, positioning my mouth near Ben's ear.

"And France must join us against the British," I whispered into Ben's ear.

"And France must join us against the British," said Ben aloud.

Vergennes nodded.

"All right, my friend," he said. "All right. Hees Majesty King Louis ees finally willing to recognize ze United States of America."

I looked at Ben. Ben looked at me. This was an incredible achievement. A king of one country had agreed to support a revolution against the king of another country! We were so happy we were practically bursting. But we couldn't show our happiness to Vergennes.

"What about joining us in our fight against the British?" I whispered in Ben's ear.

"Tell me, Monsieur Fronklin," said Vergennes. "What does ze cat do when she leans een toward your ear? Does she speak to you?"

"Speak to me?" Ben repeated, laughing uproariously at such an idea. "Of course not. Cats can't speak, you know."

"Of course cats cannot speak," said Vergennes. "And yet, sometimes thees cat seems to be wheespering to you."

Ben chuckled. "Next you're going to say the cat coaches me on what to say."

Both Ben and Vergennes laughed loudly at the idea of a cat coaching Ben Franklin on what to say.

"So tell me, Count Vergennes," said Ben when they had finished laughing. "What about joining us in our fight against the British?"

Again, Vergennes nodded, raised his eyebrows, and smiled.

"Hees Mojesty Keeng Louis ees now willing to join America een your fight against ze British."

We did it! We had gotten the only ally that we needed to win the war!

We would surely beat the British now! This never would have happened if Ben and I hadn't worked so hard on Vergennes.

CHAPTER 24

I Meet the King and Queen of France and Almost Ruin Everything

March 20, 1778. The Palace of Versailles. Ben, Benny, Temple, Silas Deane, Arthur Lee and I arrived at Versailles and got out of our carriage. We were here for the official announcement of the French-American Alliance and we were very excited.

Outside the tall iron gates of Versailles were crowds of starving French peasants dressed in filthy rags. We were sad to see their condition, but a palace servant promised to take a message inside to the queen about their lack of food.

We went through the gates onto the grounds. It was the most amazing palace I had ever seen. Actually, it was the only palace I had ever seen. There were acres and acres of flower beds and ponds and fountains. Sculptured hedges were trimmed into the shapes of bears, bulls, leopards, lions, giraffes, and hippopotamuses.

Flags snapped in the wind. Trumpets blared.

Drums rolled. Hundreds of French noblemen jammed Versailles, welcoming America as the youngest nation in the world.

Ben was thrilled. This alliance would never have been made without him. The Colonies would never have had the chance of winning the war without him. His diplomacy, his tact, and timing had made the difference.

Although Silas Deane and Arthur Lee were dressed in satin suits with lace ruffles, powdered wigs and ceremonial swords, Ben wore a poorly-fitting plain brown velvet suit, with no wig or sword.

"Grandpa, why did you wear such a shabby old suit today?" Benny asked. "It doesn't even fit you anymore."

"Benny's right," said Temple. "That brown velvet suit is so shabby, it looks like some old vagrant threw it away, because it was even too shabby for vagrants."

"Wearing this suit is my little joke on the British," Ben answered. "It's the same suit I wore in London when I was humiliated by Lord Wedderburn in the Privy Council."

"I don't understand," said Benny.

"Neither do I," said Temple. "Why would a man as famous as you wear anything so inexpensive?"

"There are many British spies here in the palace today," Ben explained. "I think they will understand my little joke."

The British spies understood Ben's joke very well indeed. "Franklin is saying he will never forgive us for humiliating him," I heard one of them whisper.

Ben, Benny, Temple, Silas Deane, Arthur Lee, and I were led to a small room with high ceilings, hung with paintings and beautiful purple velvet draperies. On a high throne sat Louis XVI, a fat, serious-looking young monarch. He shook hands with Ben and nodded to the rest of us.

"We welcome ze distinguished Americans, Dr. Fronklin and hees party," said King Louis. "We pledge ze friendsheep of France to ze United States of America."

Kings and queens never said I, they said we—it was called the royal We.

"Thank you, your Majesty," said Ben. "I know our two countries will now triumph over the British and we'll remain great friends forever."

"We have only one question," said King Louis. "Een France eet ees insulting to breeng a common poossycat to ze royal chamber. Do you now breeng thees poossycat to our chamber to insult us?"

Oh no, I thought. By bringing me to visit the king, we have destroyed our alliance with the French, the alliance we have so carefully and delicately put together. Now France will withdraw her support

from the Colonies, we will lose the war, and we'll all be hanged as traitors! I didn't want to hang! I didn't want Ben to hang! What could we do now?

"Your Majesty," said Ben, smiling, "this is a very special cat. She was bred from ancestors in Egypt and she is worth more than the finest Arabian race horse. Her name is Missy Hooper, and she never leaves my side. In America, to bring a cat to visit somebody important is the highest honor that one can pay. I bring her here today, not to insult you but to honor you."

King Louis smiled and nodded.

"Ah, well, een that case," he said, "we are honored that you have brought her here. Welcome to Versailles, Meesy Hooper, American poossycat."

I did my best to make a bow.

We were taken next to a huge drawing room in the palace. On another high throne sat Queen Marie Antoinette. She had a beautiful face, but it was so caked with makeup I wondered how she could smile or frown without her face cracking. Her white wig was so tall I was afraid it would fall off her head.

"Your Majesty," said a servant, "begging your pardon, but ze poor starving beggars outside ze gates weesh to send you a message. They say they have no more bread to eat."

"No more bread?" said Marie Antoinette. "Well then, let them eat those lovely leetle French pastries weeth ze mocha whipped cream een ze middle and ze chocolate on ze top. And now, who are these American guests?"

"May I present Dr. Fronklin, Monsieur Lee, Monsieur Deane, Monsieur Benny Fronklin, Monsieur Temple Fronklin, and ze very special American poossycat, Meessy Hooper," said the servant. "Een America eet ees not an insult to breeng a poossycat to visit someone eemportant. Eet ees ze highest honor one can pay."

"Een that case," said Marie Antoinette, "we are not insulted. Dr. Fronklin, may we scratch ze poossycat under ze chin?"

Ben looked at me. I shrugged.

"Please do," said Ben.

And so the Queen of France scratched me under my chin. How I wished my stuck-up sister Fluffy in Philadelphia could have seen me now!

Chapter 25

John Adams Won't Dance and Madame Helvetius Won't Marry

France was the first country to recognize America as a nation. France declared war on England. We knew the French were more interested in humiliating England than in winning independence for the Colonies, but we didn't care.

Ben knew the war wasn't over yet, but he didn't think it would last long now.

In 1778 Congress appointed John Adams as our first ambassador to France and sent him to help negotiate the written alliance with France.

Adams arrived with his 10-year-old son, John Quincy Adams, and their Siamese cat Frederick. Ben welcomed the Adams family to Passy and gave them rooms in our villa.

When little Johnny met little Benny, they became instant friends. It was decided to send Johnny to Benny's school. When I met Frederick, we didn't exactly become instant friends.

"Mowi rowl laurel flurr Dr. Franklin froom, croo crow frau lum-lum?" asked Frederick in Cattish. Which meant "Do you have anything to do with Dr. Franklin's work, or are you just the family lap cat?"

I couldn't believe how snotty his question was! My back went up, my ears got flat, and my tail got fat.

"Mowi merff lore rilff fffft-fffft, croo crow frau squeek-squeek-snap?" I answered. Which meant "Do you know how to speak without insults, or are you just the family mouse-trap?"

With a low growl in my throat I took a step in his direction.

Frederick was shocked. He obviously hadn't expected me to react so strongly. He stepped backward and tried to melt into the floor.

"Speak English," I said. "Unless you don't know how to do that either."

"I certainly never intended to insult you," he said, backing up some more. "If I did, I humbly apologize. I am so sorry!"

His apology was certainly humble. I unflattened my ears and unfattened my tail.

"Apology accepted," I said. "Let's start fresh. My name is Missy Hooper. Welcome to Passy."

"And I am Frederick Worthington Williams," he said. "I would appreciate it so much if you didn't call

me Freddy."

"I'll try not to," I said, "but I can't promise. I hope the French have welcomed you as warmly as they welcomed us."

"I'm afraid they haven't," said Frederick. "Do you know what they asked John Adams? 'Are you the famous Mr. Adams?' They meant his cousin, Samuel Adams."

"The one who led the Boston Tea Party," I said.

"Yes. Well, of course Mr. Adams was embarrassed and had to say no. Then they had the nerve to ask if he were Dr. Franklin's assistant." Frederick snorted with outrage. "Mr. Adams is the American ambassador to France. He is most certainly not anyone's assistant. He's a very important man in the Colonies. So important that I've been asked by the Feline Historical Society to write his biography."

"Oh, did they get to you too?" I asked. "I'm doing a biography for them of Dr. Franklin."

Frederick seemed impressed.

"You are?" he said. "How did they hear about you?"

"Oh, Ichabod Pudding used to read my work in The Philadelphia Feline."

"You wrote The Philadelphia Feline?" he asked. "Now I am impressed. Then you must also have written The London Feline and the Passy Pussy."

"That's me," I said.

"You're an excellent writer, Miss Hooper. Excellent."

"Thank you," I said, "and you can call me Missy." Well, what do you know. Maybe there was hope for this Frederick fellow after all.

"So, Ben," I said, sitting myself down on his desk and beginning a long tongue bath. "John Adams has been here for a month now. How is he doing as ambassador to France?" I raised my hind leg and started licking my belly.

"He is a complete and total disaster," Ben answered.

I looked up in surprise, forgetting my leg was still sticking up into the air.

"Really?" I said. "In what way?"

"Missy, John Adams is a Puritan. He has no social skills. I mean none. And what's more he's proud of that. He doesn't drink, dance, flirt or flatter. He disapproves of my socializing and flirting with the ladies and my entire way of doing business. You know what he wrote to Congress? 'The life of Dr. Franklin is one long party.'"

"I guess he just doesn't understand the French style," I said.

"He certainly doesn't, Missy. In the Colonies they think it's rude to look idle. In France they think it's rude to look busy. And your hind leg is still sticking up."

"Sorry."

Ben was right. John Adams worked hard, but he accomplished nothing. Ben accomplished much, but he hardly seemed to be working at all.

"Adams is just jealous of how well-known and how well-loved you are in France, Ben," I said. "He hates that you made that alliance with the French before he even got here. He thinks you and Vergennes are plotting against him. He tells the French he doesn't trust them. I mean he says that right to their faces!"

"I know," Ben sighed. "He tries to pressure Vergennes for every single thing he wants. I know when to apply pressure on Vergennes and when to pull back. Adams doesn't."

"Who ever thought he was a diplomat?" I said.

"Nobody who ever saw him in action," said Ben sadly. "When it comes to diplomacy, the man is a complete fool."

Adams was so tactless and rude that Vergennes finally refused to do business with him. Congress called Adams back to America and appointed Ben as ambassador to France. Vergennes and everyone in the French court were very relieved.

Benny and Johnny were sad to say goodbye. And I was surprisingly sorry to see Frederick go back to Philadelphia.

"Say hello to Ichabod Pudding when you see him," I said. "Tell him I'll be sending him more chapters in a few weeks."

"I will," said Frederick. "And do look me up when

you get back to Philadelphia. Perhaps we can share a bit of catnip or a chocolate-covered mouse."

At age 72, Ben was still flirting with the ladies. He fell in love with a 60-year-old widow, Madame Helvetius. "Missy," said Ben, "Madame Helvetius is not only smart and beautiful, but she also entertains famous writers, scientists and politicians in her home."

"Maybe you should ask her to marry you," I suggested.

"I did," he said. "But she knows I plan to return to America soon, and she says she's too old to move to a new country. Too old? She is just a young girl of 60! Anyway, she turned me down."

"I'm sorry, Ben," I said.

"Well, there are other lovely women in Paris," he said. "Madame Helvetius isn't the only chick in the coop."

I happen to know a lot about Madame Helvetius. Some of it good, some of it wacky. First the good: Madame Helvetius loves cats so much she has twenty of them in her house. Now the wacky: She had little embroidered fur-lined sateen jackets made for each of them to wear in cold weather. I have talked to them, and even they think cats don't need embroidered fur-lined sateen jackets. Frankly, I wasn't too upset Madame Helvetius wouldn't marry Ben.

News came to us in Passy about Ben's son William.

"William has gotten out of prison, Missy," said Ben. "He was exchanged for an American prisoner-of-war and went to New York, which is still being held by the British. He joined a band of British there, who attacked some colonists. People were killed, Missy. Innocent people. I had hoped William and I could make up someday. I now realize this is impossible."

Chapter 26

Cornwallis Changes Everything

November 19, 1781. Even with the French on our side, we were no longer winning. The French army and navy had been too slow getting into the war. The British now controlled the colonies of New York, Georgia, and South Carolina. The Americans had surrendered Charleston. Things looked hopeless. The war seemed all but lost.

Shortly after midnight on November 19, Ben was writing a letter to his daughter Sally, and I was keeping him company, lying on top of the letter. Outside it was raining hard. Freezing rain hurled itself against our window panes with every gust of wind.

Around 1:00 a.m. a rider on horseback galloped up to our door. Hoping it wasn't more bad news about the war, Ben threw on a raincoat and we ran outside to meet him.

"Sir, do you have news of the war?" Ben called

over the sound of wind and rain.

"Cornwallis!" yelled the rider breathlessly. "The Americans captured Cornwallis at Yorktown, New York!"

Ben shouted with surprise and joy. The rider got off his horse. He was dripping from the freezing rain.

"Do you know any details?" Ben asked.

"Cornwallis was running short of men, sir," said the messenger excitedly. "He was expecting help from the British navy, but the French navy cut them off and defeated them. Then Washington's army, along with the French army and the French navy and their 18,000 troops, surrounded Cornwallis and his army! The British surrendered—more than 8,000 of them!"

"When was this?" Ben yelled. A sudden gust of wind almost knocked him over.

"Exactly four weeks ago, sir, on October 19! We just got the news tonight! The British lay down their arms and walked between the French and the Colonists. The French were all grown men in military uniforms, but the Colonists were dressed in rags, and they were of all ages—farmers, grandfathers, and boys as young as 12 and 14, standing side by side, holding rifles! It was a sight to behold!"

"This changes everything, Missy!" Ben shouted to me. "This victory over Cornwallis is so dramatic, the British no longer stand a chance of winning!"

And could this have happened if Ben and I hadn't played Vergennes like a violin and gotten the French to join us? No way!

CHAPTER 27

Farts, Hot Air Balloons, Secret Negotiations, Signing a Treaty, Then Back to Philadelphia in Time to Save the Constitution and the Country

Sometime in 1781, the Royal Academy of Brussels, a famous scientific group in Belgium, asked well-known people like Ben to write scientific papers about things they felt strongly about.

"Are you going to write an essay for them?" I asked.

"I suppose so, Missy," he said, "but this academy is getting too full of itself. Too impressed with its own importance. So I'm going to write them an essay on farting."

"Hmm," I said. I thought it was a stupid idea, but I was too well-brought up to say so. "What could you possibly say about farting?" I asked.

Ben chuckled.

"I'm going to suggest that research be done into ways of improving the odor of human farts," he said. "I'm going to discuss the ways different foods affect the odor of farts and ways that this could be tested. I'm going to suggest that scientists develop a drug which could be mixed with common foods to make farts not only inoffensive, but as pleasant as perfume. I'll call my essay 'Fart Proudly.' What do you think of my idea, Missy?"

"Well, Ben," I said, "I think you ought to stick to the aphorisms."

Ben didn't agree with me. He thought his essay was the funniest thing he'd ever written. While he was writing, sometimes he laughed so hard, he dropped his quill pen, upset his ink well on the table, fell down on the floor, and gasped for breath.

"Ben, are you all right?" I would ask.

He would nod and wheeze with laughter.

I showed Ben's essay to some of my feline friends, and none of us were very amused. We cats fart all the time, but we don't see what's funny about it. We decided only human boys and 75-year-old Ben Franklin think that farts are funny.

Although he was busy negotiating a cease-fire with England, Ben never lost his interest in scientific experiments. In the southeastern part of France was one that he found particularly fascinating. The Montgolfier brothers had filled gigantic balloons with hot air, which made them able to lift human passengers more than 500 feet into the air. "Missy, this is just the start of man's ability to overcome gravity," Ben told me.

Ben hated carrying around two pairs of glasses—one for reading, another for seeing things at a distance—and continually taking one pair off and putting the other pair on. So he cut each pair of lenses into two pieces—a top half and a bottom half. He put the bottom halves of the lenses in the bottoms of the frame, and the top halves of the distance glasses in the tops of the frame. Now when he looked up he could see things far away, and when he looked down he could see things close up. He had invented bifocal glasses.

It turned out the British weren't quite ready to surrender yet. Ben contacted an old British friend from his London days, Lord Shelburne. Shelburne wanted peace and sent British representatives to negotiate with Ben.

Congress sent two men to Passy to help Ben

negotiate with the British and the French—a lawyer from New York named John Jay, and our old friend, former ambassador John Adams! Benny was delighted to see his friend Johnny again. And so was I to see Frederick. But Ben was exasperated.

"What an idiotic choice of negotiators, Missy," Ben sighed. "The French already hate Adams, and John Jay hates the French more than he does the English."

A few weeks later Ben seemed really upset. I asked what was wrong.

"Adams and Jay want to negotiate separately and secretly with England," he said.

"Why would they want to do that?" I asked.

"Because they know that France has its own selfish goals in this treaty," he said. "Eighteen years ago, the British beat France badly in the French and Indian War. France lost all the land and all the influence they'd had in North America—they wanted revenge against the British, and they wanted to regain the territory they'd lost in that war. Adams and Jay fear that in the negotiations, France's goals will endanger our most important goal—independence from England. But . . . I don't want to betray Vergennes by signing a separate treaty with England."

Ben realized that the British were willing to grant

America more in a separate treaty than they would in one that included the French. And getting the best deal from the British was the most important thing. Ben finally agreed with Adams and Jay. Together they signed the secret treaty with the British.

When Vergennes learned what Ben had done, he was very upset. But he also knew the pressure that Jay and Adams must have put on Ben.

"We must go and see Vergennes," I said. "You owe him an explanation and an apology for what you did."

"I know I do," said Ben. "But what can I possibly say to him?"

"Just tell him you know what a bad thing you did and how sorry you are."

We went to see Vergennes at his office in Paris.

"My friend," said Ben, "I was so wrong to have signed a separate treaty with the British. I don't know if you can ever forgive such a betrayal, but I apologize to you with all my heart."

Vergennes nodded, but didn't answer. I could see how hurt and angry he was. I can't say I blamed him.

"I should like to point out," said Ben, "that the treaty between the Americans and the British won't take effect until the treaty between the British and French has been signed anyway, so perhaps no harm was done."

Vergennes nodded again, but again he remained silent. I stared at Ben and shook my head. Ben was trying to excuse himself by saying what he'd done didn't matter.

"The British think they've already divided us," said Ben. "If you keep our little misunderstanding a secret, the British will find themselves mistaken."

I looked at Ben and rolled my eyes. What he'd said now was a sneaky attempt to pretend that the Americans and French were still close allies. If this weren't nervy enough, the next thing Ben did was ask Vergennes for another huge loan. And you know what? Vergennes gave it to him! I couldn't believe it!

As we were leaving the meeting room, I overheard Vergennes whisper to his secretary. "I am astonished at how much ze Americans got out of ze treaty weeth ze British," he said. "You know, ze Americans got much more by negotiating ze treaty weethout us."

The Treaty of Paris, between England and the United States of America, was officially signed on September 3, 1783. A separate treaty was signed with France. The War of Independence was finally over!

A letter arrived from William in England. Ben tore it open and read it.

"What does it say?" I asked.

"That William wants to visit me here in France," said Ben. "That he wants us to be a family again. But he refuses to admit that his actions during the war were wrong."

Ben frowned and shook his head.

"I'm going to write back saying that I would like to be a family again too, but now is not a good time to come to Paris. I shall also say that nothing has ever hurt me so much as to find myself deserted in my old age by my only son. And not only deserted, but to find him taking up arms against me in a cause where my good name, fortune, and life were at stake."

It was 1785. We had been in France for nine years. Ben was 79 years old. He told Congress he was officially retiring as ambassador and returning to Philadelphia. Thomas Jefferson, whom Ben greatly admired, would take over for him as ambassador to France.

Ben began packing. Benny helped his grandfather a teensy bit, but Temple was much too busy fussing with his own things to be of any help. If you want my opinion, Ben had spoiled Temple in the same way he spoiled William.

When we left France in July, Ben was too sick to travel by coach. King Louis XVI lent him a royal litter—a bed on wheels, pulled by mules—to travel

150 miles to the ship.

Our ship stopped briefly in England. William came to the ship to see Ben, but Ben met him on the dock next to the ship and didn't even invite him onboard. Their talk was only a cold discussion of family matters and what humans call "small talk."

"Was your crossing of the Channel a pleasant one?" asked William.

"Yes," said Ben, "quite pleasant."

"Well, you're fortunate," said William. "Sometimes it is not so pleasant. Sometimes it can get rather choppy."

"Yes, but this time it was pleasant," said Ben.

"That's good," said William.

There was an uncomfortable pause. There was no sound but the soft slap of the waves against the hull, the slight creaking of the timbers in the boat as it rode the gentle swells, and the clanging of the lines against the masts. I saw Ben sneak a look at his pocket watch.

"Well, I hope that your crossing of the Atlantic will be equally pleasant," said William when the silence became unbearable.

"Oh, I'm sure that there will be some rough weather on the Atlantic crossing," said Ben, "but the rest of it should be rather pleasant."

"Yes," said William.

Cat fathers and their grown kittens aren't any warmer than that to each other, but I somehow expected more from humans.

William wasn't very warm to either Temple or Benny either, but maybe that was because they hadn't seen one another for nine years. Ben and William parted without any warmth or affection at all. They just shook hands. They didn't hold each other's hand for long and they didn't squeeze it. They could have been total strangers who'd met once at a party. That made me sad.

It was the last time that Ben and William would ever see each other.

Chapter 28

At Age 81, Ben Saves the Constitution but Not Himself

On the voyage back to America Ben continued his study of the long, wide, river-in-the-ocean he'd discovered that warms much of Europe and the Eastern part of America. It would later be known as the Gulf Stream. Ben tied a thermometer to a long string and kept dropping it into the water and taking the ocean's temperature.

"This band of water is warmer than the ocean around it, Missy," he said. "It also appears to grow more weeds, and whales don't seem to like swimming in it."

"I have a new aphorism for you," I said. "'A warm river gathers neither weeds nor whales.'"

He frowned and shook his head. "Not to hurt your feelings, Missy, but I don't think you ever got the hang of making aphorisms," he said.

When we returned to America, Ben announced his retirement. But America had other plans for him. Ben was elected President of the Pennsylvania Assembly.

The Continental Congress was still holding meetings, but it had no power. The 13 states weren't getting along with each other.

Ben was frustrated and angry.

"The states are acting like they're separate countries," he said to me in disgust. "They're making laws the other states don't like. They're even printing their own money. Their debts are huge, but each state has its own system of money, and most states' paper money is worth almost nothing. We can't call this The United States of America. To be truthful, we'll have to call it The Completely Separate States of America Who Can't Agree on Anything at All."

"That will never fit on the money," I said.

The leaders of the Constitutional Congress knew they needed a plan for a new central government, and fast—one that would be stronger than the separate states. A Constitutional Convention was organized in Philadelphia in May 1787. Along with seven other men, Ben was elected to represent the state of Pennsylvania.

"The small states are afraid of the power of the big ones, Missy," Ben told me. "Some states want a president who'll be as strong as a king. Some states want a president who'll have hardly any power. But 55 men are still trying to build a government."

Somehow, an American Constitution got written—don't ask me how. But when it was voted on, neither side had won a majority. The vote was deadlocked.

Ben and I sat with the 54 other delegates in the large, high-ceilinged convention hall with its wooden tables and benches that had been made so recently that you could still smell the fresh odor of pine. The disappointment and the resentment of the delegates in the room was so strong you could smell that too.

"Unless a majority of the delegates vote in favor of this draft of the Constitution, Missy," Ben whispered to me, "there will be no Constitution at all. And if there isn't a Constitution, there will be no United States of America. Everything that we have fought for, everything that we have won, will be lost forever. The whole thing will have been in vain."

"Why don't you try one more time to get them to agree?" I said.

He shook his head.

"I am 81 years old, Missy," he said. "I'm not at all well. I'm so sick I can barely speak."

What Ben said was true. His voice sounded cracked and hoarse, as if it had been used way too

much and just finally broken down.

"But they need your advice, Ben," I whispered. "They respect you. They'll listen to whatever you have to say. You must try to speak to them."

"I no longer have a voice loud enough to even get their attention," he said.

It was true. I could barely hear him myself, and I was sitting on his lap.

"I will tell someone from the Pennsylvania

delegation to announce that you have something important to say," I whispered. "Will you speak to them then?"

He shrugged and sighed.

"It won't do any good," he said. "They are all good men, but they're as stubborn as mules. I know them. They will never change their minds."

"Ben," I pleaded, "if you don't say anything now, then all is lost for sure. But if you try to reason with them, there's at least a chance that some of them may decide to change their votes. All you need to do is convince just one of them to change. Isn't that worth a try?"

He nodded.

"You're right, dear friend," he said, scratching me under the chin.

"It is better to try and fail than merely to sit on your tail," I said.

Ben groaned.

"Better leave the aphorisms to me," he said.

"Sorry," I said.

I tapped a Pennsylvania delegate named James Wilson on the shoulder with my paw. He turned around and looked at me.

"Ben would like to address the convention," I said. "Would you please let them know that?"

I had never talked to James Wilson before, so

that's probably why his mouth flopped open when I began to speak.

"D-did you just speak to me?" he asked.

"Yes," I said. "Sorry if I startled you, but this is important. Ben would like to address the convention. Would you let them know that?"

James Wilson turned to look at Ben.

Ben smiled at him and nodded.

James Wilson tried to compose himself. Then he rapped on the table with an empty inkwell for silence.

"Sorry to interrupt, gentlemen," he said, "but I have just been informed by . . . an associate of Dr. Franklin that he would like to address this convention."

Everyone turned to look at Ben. Then they began to applaud.

Ben smiled at the applause. Then, leaning on his cane, he rose shakily to his feet.

"My dear friends," he croaked. "I would like to say something, but . . . I am old, and my voice is weak. If you cannot hear me . . . I apologize. You may ask your neighbors what I have said."

He paused to take several deep breaths. It was so quiet in the hall, you could have heard a mouse sneeze. As a matter of fact, I did I hear a mouse sneeze.

Ben continued.

"Unless a majority of us delegates vote in favor of this draft of the Constitution," Ben said, "there will be no Constitution at all. And if there is no Constitution . . . there will be no United States of America. Everything that we have fought for, everything that we have won, will be . . . lost forever. And all of the brave colonists who fought and died in our revolution . . . will have died in vain."

Ben had a brief fit of coughing, and then he continued.

"I consent to this Constitution," he told the convention, his voice weak, barely loud enough to hear. "It may not be perfect, but . . . I think it may be the best. And although we may all have some objections to it, let us . . . put those aside now and . . . make our vote unanimous."

He sat down heavily and seemed to be short of breath. All of the delegates were chattering among themselves.

The delegates took another vote. This time they voted to adopt the Constitution.

Ben smiled at me and winked. I licked his hand.

Ben's very last job was as president of a group urging an end to slavery in the United States, but their petition was rejected by Congress.

Ben Franklin was the only person to have signed

the four documents that created the United States—
the Declaration of Independence, the wartime treaty
with France, the peace treaty with England, and the
Constitution.

On April 17, 1790, Ben died at the age of 84. I
was with him at his bedside. He smiled at me and
squeezed my paw. I licked his face.

In France, the National Assembly, the French
senate, voted to wear black clothes and shut down
for three days to mourn his death. The French Royal
Society of Medicine declared, "A man is dead, and
two worlds are in mourning."

In Philadelphia there were 20,000 people—nearly
half of the city—at his funeral. At his request Ben
was buried beside his wife Debby.

Goodbye, dear friend. I will miss you terribly.

A note to the reader: I finished this biography
for Ichabod Pudding four months after Ben's death.
It should give you a much more accurate picture of
what Ben was really like than any account written
by a human. If you have been reading this story in
English, I urge you to try and get it from the Feline
Historical Society in the original Cattish, because
there are certain expressions that simply lose a lot in
the translation.

Cattish Vocabulary

Browr: Wants
Croo: Or
Crow: Just
Fffft: Mad
Fffft-fffft: Insults
Flurr: To do with
Frau: Family
Froom: Work
Gracko: Congratulations
Laurel: Anything
Lore: To speak
Lum-lum: Lap-cat
Mee: You
Meer: Who
Meer browr merff?: Who wants to know?
Mel: Can
Meow: Hello, goodbye or peace
Merff: To know

Merl: This
Merow: Be sure
Mowi: Do you
Mowr: I was
Muffer: Luck
Per: Good
Per muffer: Good luck
Pert: Me
Prim: Really
Prowl: I'm better
Rare: Feeling upset.
Rilff: Without
Row: How
Rowl: Have
Snap: Trap
Squeek-squeek: Mouse
Yaw: Feed me NOW
Yawoo: Scares

BENJAMIN FRANKLIN TIMELINE

1706, January 17: Ben is born in a house on Milk Street in Boston, Massachusetts.

1714: Ben starts grammar school.

1716: Ben is taken out of school, apprenticed to his father, a soap and candle maker.

1718: Ben is apprenticed to brother James, a printer.

1722: Ben writes letters to newspaper, becomes famous as Silence Dogood.

1723: Ben, age 17, runs away from James and Boston, moves to Philadelphia.

1724: Ben, age 18, sails to London, works as a printer.

1726: Ben, age 20, gets homesick, moves back to Philadelphia.

1729: Ben buys a failing newspaper, The Pennsylvania Gazette.

1730: Ben, age 24, marries Deborah Read, has a

son, William.

1731: Ben starts first public library.

1732: Ben and Debby have a son, Franky. Ben starts Philadelphia's first police department, first hospital, first college, first volunteer fire department. He presses Philadelphia to pave its streets, starts Philadelphia's first sanitation department. He starts Poor Richard's Almanac.

1736: Four-year-old Franky dies in a smallpox epidemic. Ben is appointed Clerk of the Pennsylvania Assembly, forms the Union Fire Company of Philadelphia.

1737: Ben is appointed Deputy Postmaster-General of Philadelphia, elected to the Assembly, plans a city police department.

1738: Ben begins to study French, Italian, Spanish, and Latin.

1742: Ben invents the Franklin stove, refuses to patent it.

1743: Ben and Debby have a daughter, Sally. Ben gets idea to create the University of Pennsylvania.

1748: Ben, age 42, is rich. He sells his printing business and retires to pursue science and have fun. He invents first commercial fertilizer, identifies lead poisoning, experiments with electricity.

1751: Ben helps found a hospital.

1752: Ben flies a kite in a storm and proves

lightning and electricity are the same.

1753: Ben, age 47, invents the lightning rod, is named Postmaster of the six Northern Colonies, receives an M.A. degree from both Yale and Harvard. He is now the most famous American in the world.

1754: The Colonial Congress at Albany, NY, appoints him a Commissioner from Pennsylvania; he proposes a plan for the union of the colonies.

1755: Helps establish a voluntary army to protect the colonists from Indian attacks, is given the rank of Colonel, leads his troops to build a fort.

1757: Ben is sent to London to get the Penn family to pay taxes on its land in Pennsylvania.

1759: St. Andrews University awards Ben an honorary Doctor of Laws degree, from now on he is addressed as Dr. Franklin.

1760: The Penns are finally forced to pay taxes.

1762: Ben gets son William appointed governor of New Jersey. Ben receives degrees from Oxford and Edinburgh. After five years in England, he returns to America.

1764: Ben returns to London to represent the Colonies' interests as agent for Pennsylvania.

1765: Parliament passes The Stamp Act, the Colonies rebel.

1770, March 5: The Boston Massacre.

1773, December 16: The Boston Tea Party.

1774, January 27: Ben is humiliated in the Privy Council, becomes a revolutionary. Ben's wife Debby dies.

1775: Ben returns to America after 10 years. Battles of Lexington and Concord.

1776, July 4: Ben is a co-author and co-signer of the Declaration of Independence.

October 29: Ben, age 70, goes to France to get her as an ally against England.

1777: New York and Philadelphia captured by British, but Colonists defeat General Burgoyne at Saratoga. The French join the Colonists against the British.

1778, March 20: The French formally recognize America, join us against the British. Ben, age 72, falls in love with Madame Helvetius, asks her to marry him, she says no.

1781, October19: George Washington, along with the French army and navy, surround the British army at Yorktown, Virginia. Cornwallis and 8,000 British soldiers surrender.

1783, September 3: The Treaty of Paris is signed, and the War of Independence is over.

1785, July: Ben, age 79, returns to America after nine years in France, is elected President of the Pennsylvania Assembly.

1787, May: A Constitutional Convention is organized in Philadelphia. Ben, age 81, is elected with seven other men to represent Pennsylvania.

1788: Ben retires from public life.

1790, April 17: Ben dies at the age of 84. There are 20,000 people at his funeral.

Author's Note

All events, facts, and characters described in this book, including Franklin's more obscure inventions and his essay on flatulence, are absolutely true, excluding the presence of, and actual quotes from, certain Feline Americans.

SOURCES

A Partial Bibliography

Blum, John M.; McFeeley, William S.; Morgan, Edmund S.; Schlesinger, Arthur M., Jr.; Stampp, Kenneth M.; Woodward, C. Vann, <u>The National Experience: A History of the United States.</u> San Diego: Harcourt Brace Jovanovich, 1985.

Brands, H.W., <u>The First American: The Life and Times of Benjamin Franklin.</u> New York: Anchor Books, 2002.

Coss, Stephen, "What Led Benjamin Franklin to Live Estranged from His Wife for Nearly Two Decades?" <u>Smithsonian Magazine</u>, September, 2017.

Davis, Kenneth C., <u>Don't Know Much About History.</u> New York: Avon/Crown, 1995.

Ellis, Joseph J., <u>Founding Brothers.</u> New York: Vintage Books, 2000.

Franklin, Benjamin, <u>The Autobiography of Benjamin Franklin</u>. Hollywood, FL: Simon & Brown, 2010.

Franklin, Benjamin, <u>Fart Proudly: Writings of Benjamin Franklin You Never Read in School.</u> Marble Hill, GA: Enthea Press, 2003.

Isaacson, Walter, <u>Benjamin Franklin, An American Life.</u> New York: Simon & Schuster, 2003.

Johnson, Robert D., Ph.D., <u>The Making of America.</u> Washington, D.C.: National Geographic Society, 2002.

Rubel, David and Weinstein, Allen, <u>The Story of America.</u> London: Agincourt Press/DK, 2002.

www.ingramcontent.com/pod-product-compliance
Lightning Source LLC
Chambersburg PA
CBHW070140080526
44586CB00015B/1768